Rancho La Puerta is especially thankful for its many guests over the years who have chronicled their Ranch experiences through photography. Many of their photos appear in this book.

The cover is from a painting by the late
Mexican artist Aurelio Pescina.
Color photographs by John Durant.

Library of Congress Catalog Number 89-092690
International Standard Book Number: ISBN 0-9625089-O-X

F ifty years of memories…
of family and of hundreds of thousands of guests…
I dedicate this work to my late husband,
Edmond Szekely, the visionary who led us
to this wondrous place, and to my parents,
Rebecca and Harry Shainman,
who put me on the path.

Deborah Szekely

THY FOOD SHALL
BE THE REMEDY

—Hippocrates c 460-377 B.C.

Dining room staff, mid 1950's

A SPECIAL NOTE OF APPRECIATION TO OUR
PRESENT AND GREATEST CHEF
Bill Wavrin

AND TO THE GIFTED COLLABORATION OF
Chef Joseph D. Cochran
Chef Tracy Ritter and
Nutritionist Leona Marie Fitzgerald

Contents

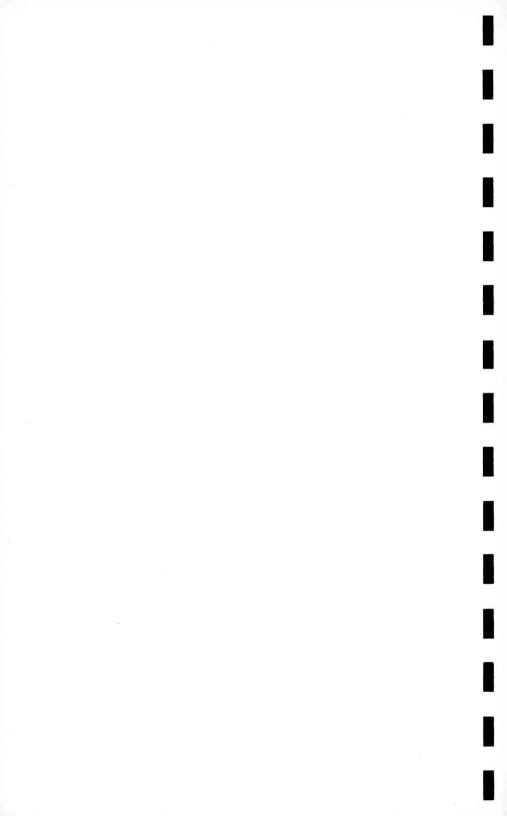

Forward

BY DEBORAH SZEKELY

Morning. My mountain hike complete, I look forward to breakfast. In fact, I'm ravenous—like everyone else who has experienced the vigor of rising before the sun begins its own climb up the bouldered slopes of Mt. Kuchumaa. Perhaps a slice of cantaloupe and rich, creamy papaya. The nutty crumble of toasted Ranch bread and smooth, sour-sweet homemade yogurt with a bit of local honey.

Sitting outside on the olive grove-shaded patios of Rancho La Puerta's dining hall, even in the brisk but still-temperate days of winter, I begin my daily celebration of foods healthfully prepared: Simple—yet imaginative, zestful, and immensely satisfying.

As I eat quietly, legs still tingling from Kuchumaa's winding paths, I know that others are already at work in the garden Tres Estrellas. Located not far up the valley, it is where we grow many of our vegetables, berries, herbs and fruits in rich, sandy soil—pure,

Fresh from our organic garden, vegetables are celebrated in eye-appealing dishes.

deep alluvium washed into this basket of a valley by a millennia of brief winter storms that have prowled the Laguna crest and left their pure waters for our wells.

One of the chefs is picking rosemary from a bed beside the patio, and the sharp, distinctly Mediterranean smell drifts past me. A few dark, ripe olives nestle in the joints between the tiles, escapees from a picking last week when Enrique and his staff filled dozens of baskets for another pressing of our own olive oil.

Already our guests are out and about, heading to class, stopping for a quick sip of tea in the pavilion, laughing, talking quietly…striding, up on their toes, breathing. Fueled by the diet of the Ranch, they embark on a day filled with exercise, stretching, yoga, meditation, massage—wherever their spirit and energy take them. Extraordinary, even to the most fit, is the way this energy has been building for days. Are they "dieting?" Not really. They are eating the way we were always meant to eat, and their bodies are responding, opening once more to the possibilities of being fully alive.

Now in my seventh decade, the food of Rancho La Puerta excites and energizes me as much as it ever did. More, even! Perhaps the biggest change has been in presentation, for we've learned that food can be beautiful while remaining true to its carefully tended origins (in this regard we owe much to the Japanese). It is a feast for the eyes as well as the tummy, and I confess that though we tried mightily in the early days of the Ranch, things looked—well—simpler then.

As I review this collection of recipes from the many years of Ranch cooking, dating all the way back to when I was the chef in the early 1940s, I'm struck with the way we've stayed true to some fundamental principles that others "discovered" decades later. While some proponents of healthy diets wandered the entire map of cuisines and fads, we have embraced whole grains and legumes since the beginning. What has truly changed is variety. We grow a dozen or more lettuces now, compared to one or two in the early days, but they all still saw the sunrise in their warm Tres Estrellas beds. Asparagus thrives in our dry, sunny climate. We press our own olive oil and imbue it with many flavors, but it is just another chapter in our long saga of making as much of our own food as possible. And why not? It tastes better. It is worth the effort.

"Now in my seventh decade, the food of Rancho La Puerta excites and energizes me as much as it ever did."

As guests arrived in greater and greater numbers at our door—our *puerta*—they still brought with them their notions that a "meal" was nothing more than meat and potatoes, salt and pepper. Their idea of an exotic herb was dill. Basil was too strong. Oh how awareness has changed! Today we embrace stronger flavors. We appreciate the toothy snap of a gently cooked bean rather than wondering if it's "undercooked."

Truly, food has been a vital part of the Ranch since its inception. It has shaped my own life. Nurtured me. Taught me more than I could have ever hoped.

And to think it began with a dusty ride through a small town called Tecate...

x

On Christmas day, 1939, I, a 17-year-old Brooklyn-born girl, became the bride of Edmond Szekely, a 34-year-old Hungarian scholar, philosopher and natural-living experimenter. Through a chain of extraordinary circumstances, the following summer we hosted a small but fascinating international clientele at a health camp hastily assembled at Tecate, Baja California. At that time Tecate was a secluded Mexican border village of 400 inhabitants just across the international line, chosen by my husband for having the finest year-round climate in North America.

On June 6, 1940, I rolled down a Tecate dirt road in our 12-year-old Cadillac—vintage and still a touch elegant with its plush interior and, at the windows, cut-crystal bud vases. Fastened to the car's rear trunk and bumper were all our worldly possessions, packed in a single silver-painted wooden box. The car was a wedding gift from one of the happy participants in a previous health camp Edmond had conducted at Rio Corona in Tamaulipas, Mexico.

Rancho La Puerta "Home Sweet Home"

Experienced and indefatigable in his chosen specialization, Edmond had directed and learned from natural-living experiments at Nice, France; Tahiti; Lake Elsinore, California; Rio Corona, in the Mexican state of Tamaulipas; Leatherhead, Surrey, England; Spanish Town, Jamaica; and Uruapan in the Mexican state of Michoacán. It was in Tahiti that he first met my family, fruitarians who had chosen to ride out the Great Depression's early years by escaping to what was still a true tropical paradise. Thereafter, my parents, together with their young children (my brother and me), attended and actively supported his projects, wherever they might take us.

The Cadillac brought me to join my husband at what we supposed would be another temporary living/learning venture. For $10 a month he rented a one-room adobe hut sitting in the middle of a vineyard called Rancho La Puerta. That seemed like a lot of money to us then, since the war in Europe had cut off my husband's income.

Rocks were used to keep the roof down and barbed wire to keep the cows away. A wood-burning stove was used for cooking.
My dream gift for Christmas 1941 was a gasoline iron.

After pulling up in front of the Tecate adobe and learning that our new house had a dirt floor, holes for windows and door, and consisted of a single room 10- by 30-feet wide, I could hardly hold back my tears.

Rancho La Puerta—the Beginning

We soon discovered that until our arrival the adobe hut had been used to store hay. Cattle who believed there was still food inside noisily rubbed up against the walls at night.

There was precious little time for tears or annoying night sounds, since the arrival of the first year's guests was imminent. We hastily planted lettuce, green onions, radishes, and tomatoes, using the organic farming methods my husband had learned from Sir Albert Howard's Agricultural Testament. From a neighboring rancher we purchased a goat. This was to be the first of many: By 1943 we were milking 90 goats and offering fresh goat cheese to guests.

Our camp's policy was one of absolute simplicity: $17.50 per week; bring your own tent; no running water; no electricity; neither gym nor swimming pool; but a great mountain (historically called Mount Kuchumaa by the Indians, it appears on U.S. maps as Tecate Peak) for climbing, plus a river for swimming; goats for milk and cheese; an exciting organic vegetable garden—the West Coast's first, yielding a generous harvest.

The Essenes—Our Guiding Light

It would be several years before our camp would revert to its Spanish land-grant name, Rancho La Puerta. At the start we called it the Essene School of Life because, long before the revelations of the Dead Sea Scrolls, my husband had minutely studied the sect of the ancient Essenes and their Dead Sea colony. At the time of Christ they were teaching a kindly philosophy and leading a practical, peaceful life. They were, as my husband explained in his books and lectures, the world's first great agriculturists and natural healers.

The Essene Science of Life
INTRODUCTION TO COSMOTHERAPY
SECOND EDITION

•

PROF. DR. EDMOND SZEKELY

Youth—Vitality—Longevity
MODERN SCIENTIFIC DIET
⋯ING—BATHING

Until the 1950s and the discovery of the Dead Sea Scrolls, the Essenes were an obscure part of history. They eventually were elevated to their rightful place in the early hierarchy of the Holy Land.

Prophecy Fulfilled

Daily, our guests enthusiastically listened to Edmond (the Professor, as he was affectionately called) lecture on the rules for vibrant good health, long life, and a caring philosophy that recognized the interdependence of mind, body, and spirit. They then lived those rules 24 hours a day.

The thrust of my husband's message was amazingly prophetic. He warned against herbicides, pesticides, and artificial fertilizers. He criticized food processing and packaging. He emphasized the dangers of cigarettes and alcohol and the crucial need for pure air and pure water. He pinpointed the exact rules now advocated for safe sunbathing and proper absorption of Vitamin D. Long before the Korean War he recognized the potential threat of cholesterol and fats in the American diet.

Our pioneering Rancho La Puerta menu was exemplary, revolutionary, and wonderfully simple. Breakfast was fresh raw milk from our goats, whole-grain bread from grain which we grew and germinated, and wild-sage honey. Luncheon often consisted of cheese from our own goat milk, a ripe home-grown tomato, sprouted wheat with watercress and green sprouts from our sprouting room. Legumes were almost always the main dish at dinner. With it we usually served a whole-grain cereal, an ear of corn or a baked potato, green salad, and fresh fruit for dessert. Most of this vegetarian bounty came from our own camp, just as the gardens and orchards at both Rancho La Puerta and the Golden Door supply our guests today.

Summer, 1940, and for several years afterward, everyone chopped and carried firewood. Everyone performed farm chores. Everyone took part in the do-everything-from-scratch kitchen detail. Nobody complained too much about "having the duty"—taking the goats onto the hills.

"Daily our guests enthusiastically listened to the Professor lecture on the rules for vibrant good health, long life and a caring philosophy…"

Deborah Szekely in 1941, Rancho La Puerta

Besides assisting my husband with supervisory details, I also ground wheat, watered sprouts, and made cheese and the beds.

I would certainly have set the communal table, had we possessed one. Instead, we tagged every plate and placed it on a shelf in a large bin, and guests retrieved their own. They then went to eat alone in some choice Nature spot free from interruption. We encouraged them to reflect while they ate and to consider all the vitality this simple natural food would supply—enhancing their oneness with Nature and giving meaning to the Cosmos that they absorbed with each breath and mouthful. Today you would call it Meditation.

To inspire positive thoughts we gave our guests cards on which were printed the Essene Communions with our Earthly Mother and Heavenly Father. Everyone was to focus on the special communion for the day.

The Essene School early 1940s — lunch ingredients similar to today's, only presentation differs.

As I look over several 1943 cards, I see some messages were in the realm of simple thanksgiving and celebration:

The heavenly Father and I are one.

The Earthly Mother and I are one.
She gives the food of life to my whole body.

The Angle of power descends upon my acting body and directs my acts.

The Angel of sun enters my solar point and gives the fire of life to my whole body.

The Angel of water enters my blood and gives the water of life to my whole body.

The Angel of wisdom descends upon my thinking body and enlightens all my thoughts.

Some were supplications:

Angel of work, descend upon humanity and give abundance to all men.

Angel of joy, descend upon the earth and give beauty to all beings.

Many communions anticipated present-day biofeedback and other recent techniques for bringing into focus certain parts of the body:

Intensifying and directing metabolism of the body:
Contemplating edible fruits, grains or plants.

Absorbing by our acting body (nervous system) cosmovital forces from the stars:
Contemplating stars, their radiations and the cosmic ocean of life.

Radiating and directing accumulated solar forces from the solar plexus:
Contemplating the rising sun.

En masse, participants at our first Ranch camps joined us at dawn for a meditation hike up our mountain to greet the Morning Sun. At sundown we paid a similar tribute to the Evening Star.

Whenever I look back upon those early days, it seems to me that Rancho La Puerta must have been predestined. How else to explain its survival in a place (at that time) only slightly less inaccessible than Ultima

Thule, in a world preoccupied with history's most widespread war? Travel restrictions before long prevented many of our faithful United Kingdom friends from revisiting our Essene School of Life. Obviously, we needed to make a bridge to the world.

Spreading the News

To inform, to educate, to celebrate all that was going on, we established a monthly newsletter: $10 for 12 issues a year. Subscribers to our mind/body fitness bulletin also were privileged to receive individual advice in response to their write-in questions. By the end of W.W.II, we counted over a hundred members in half a dozen countries who ensured that our annual six-week summer school was oversubscribed.

To turn out the monthly newsletter, my husband would lecture or dictate in French or Esperanto; I would translate, type, and cut stencils. Guests helped out with the mimeograph machine which we set up under the oak tree (the "Ranch of the Door" was named for two arching trees; the shell of one still exists and is very much alive, a testament to the tenacity of nature). The bulletin was crucial in enabling my husband to continue his work. Within a few years it provided the wherewithal for acquiring our own small printing press, and its revenues contributed to the physical growth of the Essene School of Life.

"Cosmos, Man and Society", written in 1936

Besides turning out a many-paged bulletin once a month, Edmond also wrote a large number of books and pamphlets. After an English publishing house brought out his world view, *Cosmos, Man and Society*, when Edmond was only 33, he continued to amplify what many consider his master work. As a Renaissance man who read in eight languages, he drew information from all that was new in philosophy, science, and medicine. At the same time he reached back to retrieve the great verities of antiquity. Rancho La Puerta fuses all he admired in the ancient and modern worlds. In addition to the many

COSMOS,
MAN AND SOCIETY
A Paneubiotic Synthesis

By
EDMOND SZÉKELY

Translated and Edited by
L. PURCELL WEAVER

With drawings by
ARTHUR WRAGG

W. DANIEL COMPANY LTD.
England.

pamphlets on the Essenes, Edmond's other subject groups included the humanities and scholarly comparative studies of religions.

He also wrote about herb uses when they were nearly forgotten, and about vitamins and minerals before their RDA's were well-known.

The young people of the 1960s revived interest in his works. His books are proving to be equally relevant to 1990s' youth.

Nurturing the Mental and Physical

You who are familiar with Rancho La Puerta, the 1990s fitness-spa showplace...over 75 handsome casitas (little homes in the Mexican Colonial mode with fireplaces and flower bedecked patios)... 300 acres, of which 50 are landscaped...full resort facilities...would tend to smile at the pride which we felt as the number of guest tents multiplied, and one by one we added first wood and then brick buildings.

As the camp increased in size and amenities and extended to year-round, we found it attracting another type of guest. Word got out that pounds could be shed on our well-balanced vegetarian diet, which was even then low in calories, fat, salt, and cholesterol, and totally eschewed refined white sugar and flour.

"As the camp increased in size and amenities and extended to year-round, we found it attracting another type of guest."

By 1950, 10 years after we welcomed our first guests with our initial charge of $17.50, our rates had escalated to the vast sum of $25 per week.

From Day One I was secretary, chef, housekeeper and Activities/Exercise Director. At its most primitive, early 1940s level, my day consisted of trying to cope with 35 guests underfoot who interrupted my other work. That's when I first began to make up guest schedules, the original ones being such basic directives as, "Sunbathe briefly at 10 A.M...Work in the garden for one hour before the midday sun." I was inadvertently establishing the pattern of today's spa schedule, in which an active class period invariably follows one of passive exercise or rest.

My husband's lectures were always the highlight of every guest's day. Nevertheless, I found that guests who

1955 Ranch mailer pictured stone-quarried pool, library and new vineyard dining room.

might miss a lecture would turn up in time for calisthenics. Realizing guest's needs, I turned more and more to exercise.

Since the lectures ventured into profundity, I resolved to lighten up the exercise periods—and increase them.

Reviewing the calisthenics common at that time, I could see that they were often boring. I inserted games into exercise, or silly rhymes and, most of all, music. Neighbor children thought it was great fun to hand-crank a portable-phonograph accompaniment for a few cents an hour and the opportunity to learn English from our guests.

I had not yet started a family of my own, and the Ranch and its guests (and the residents we gradually hired to assist us) became in a sense my surrogate children. I fretted over guests especially as I tried to analyze what they wanted and what they thought they needed, as opposed to what they probably should have.

Transcending Boundaries

While I was restructuring our exercise program, my husband was experimenting with some very old and valid health theories, principally the hydrotherapy recommendations of Father Sebastian Kneipp. Our adaptation of Kneipp's herbal wrap became a regular Ranch treatment because it eased muscular soreness caused by unaccustomed exercise.

During that experimental period my husband became intrigued with solar heating (then very new), which he used successfully in our first bath house, dedicated with proud fanfare in the early 1950s. We also cooked often with solar power, employing his complex concoction of highly polished sheets of stainless steel. And our

Mud baths, herbal wraps, sunbathing... we put the skin in touch with Nature.

replica *temezcal* (Aztec version of the sauna), heated with a wood fire during winter, converted to solar heat in summer.

Eventually we learned that the novelties which made a difference in the lives of our new guests were those that supplied what the guests had been most lacking—adequate movement and proper nutrition.

My husband's gift for carrying in his head an elaborate panoramic view of both the modern and ancient worlds of course influenced our total approach to the Ranch's Health Day. To calisthenics we soon added Hatha Yoga, at a time when the West tended to regard all the 16 Yoga disciplines as bizarrely transcendental and linked to Eastern religion.

Hatha Yoga, the yoga of physical activity, interested us because of its enormous variety. It relaxed the tense Americans who were replacing the early pilgrims who had hauled water, stacked firewood, chased after goats, baked bread in a Mexican outdoor oven, lent a hand in our first makeshift office, and hoed weeds in the vineyard.

Chef/Baker María Rivera, 1945. She retired from Rancho La Puerta in 1980.

The Fitness Revolution Begins

Soon I was hiring instructors with backgrounds in modern dance. For many years we trained such teachers and they formed the cadre from which all of today's fitness-spa instruction springs. Now universities have augmented phys-ed courses with this sort of training, and we are able to hire staff who come to us with fitness degrees.

Assembling as many activities as possible (this is now called cross-training and is much in vogue) and continuing to alternate each active class with a passive one, we offered our guests a myriad of participatory choices: special hikes each morning up mystic Mount Kuchumaa, exercising in water, relaxing in Yoga stretch classes, playing volleyball on land and in water, walking and dancing to rousing music with a strong beat. Exercise to jazz was voted the most popular class of the day.

All this was the genesis of our Health Day, the basis of every present-day spa program.

We monitored our guests and faithfully charted their progress. Before they left, we suggested a home program which they could adjust to their daily living.

Aldous Huxley, Rancho La Puerta, 1959

Little by little we "graduated" guests who took full advantage of all the opportunities implicit in a Rancho La Puerta vacation, adhering to their take-home guidelines, returning annually for "refresher courses," and following the lead of the Ranch, as we in turn closely followed all that was most current, promising, and appropriate in the diet-exercise, mind-body fitness-health field. These people were the torchbearers of the Fitness Revolution which Rancho La Puerta gestated, nurtured, and introduced to the world.

Birth of "The Door"

Throughout the late 1940s and early 1950s, among the Ranch's cum laude graduates was a sizeable delegation from what is often called the Golden Age of Motion Pictures. These directors and performers applauded our development from a small primitive fitness camp to a large rustic resort improving its program from year to year. But our Hollywood friends yearned for more privacy and intimacy than the Ranch could guarantee. Some of them talked to me of the possibility of a similar spa with smaller capacity and greater exclusivity.

The Golden Door in Escondido, California (about an hour north of San Diego), became the recipient of all the empirical knowledge and health resort know-how we had researched and demonstrated at the Ranch. But it went beyond its sister spa in Mexico by offering extravagant TLC in a luxurious setting as pleasing as Nature—and a committed human effort—could possibly make it.

One of the factors that led me to select our site in the Escondido countryside is that it affords "Door" guests their very own mountain for the same ritual Dawn walk so loved at the Ranch.

"But our Hollywood friends yearned for more privacy and intimacy than the Ranch could guarantee."

We founded the Golden Door in 1958, and in 1960 observed Rancho La Puerta's 20th anniversary. The celebration was in keeping with our mission: a seminar on the Human Potential—the first use of that glowing term—featuring Aldous Huxley and other prominent thinkers of that day. Ten years later we welcomed our 30th anniversary with a seminar put together by Gardner Murphy.

In 1990 we reaffirmed the Human Potential with a 50th Year celebration planned through June 1991.

Over the last three decades the Ranch and the Golden Door have been like very close, very fond sisters who continually compare notes—and profit from each other's successful experiences.

Nutrition and Spa Cuisine

From its inception, the "Door" always observed my husband's Ranch-proven rules of nutrition and depended upon fresh, organically-grown foods. It differed from the Ranch by serving fresh fish and occasional range-fed chicken (NO red meat) and, most significantly, in initiating the idea of decalorized Continental Cuisine (in other words, Spa Food).

The recipes in this book often mirror our well-known heritage of Spa Food haute cuisine. (For, just as the Ranch has steadily grown more beautiful, so too it has taken inspiration from the Golden Door kitchen by presenting meals of greater variety and sophistication.) But you will also recognize in the recipes a number of wholesome comfort foods so traditional to the Ranch but now hailed everywhere as a new cuisine trend.

Joy in eating and joy in exercise are integral to both our family spas. No sincere explanation of our suggestions for healthful food planning would be complete without urging a comparable plan for daily exercise. Diet alone cannot assure a fit and slender body, lasting vitality, and the natural high that can transform you and your personal world.

"…to survive in this increasingly artificial world, mankind will have to reprise old ways of eating nutritiously and moving naturally… all in all leading to a useful, long healthful life"

Those people who achieve their ideal weight and hold to it are the ones who have rejected the sedentary existence and fitted themselves with a pattern of systematically scheduled exercise which they not only can endure but actually enjoy. Walking or swimming or joining a gym class—whatever your choice, it must be practical; it must suit your taste as well as the exigencies of your daily life.

That has been the message which Rancho La Puerta and the Golden Door impress upon our guests. Neither spa has ever veered from the late Edmond Szekely's essential philosophy: A belief that, to survive in this increasingly artificial world, mankind will have to reprise old ways of eating nutritiously and moving naturally, and in so doing will establish new ways of achieving balance and realizing one's entire potential…all-in-all leading to a useful, long, healthful life.

Keepers of the Flame

There must be a kind of conservator gene which the Szekely children have inherited, for they have followed in the footsteps of my grandparents and parents, who were innkeepers, and my husband and me, who instilled in them a healthy respect for Nature.

Our son Alex always knew exactly what he wished his life work to be: Running the two spas and taking care of our guests. Years before he assumed full charge, I could see that he would excel at his chosen profession. After a summer as a bellhop when he was about 12, he asked my secretary to type a memo which began, "I don't see why the guests have to wait until I take over, for them to enjoy what I know should be done."

Our daughter Livia is the artist-poet-musician of the family. Her love for people and for the flora and fauna of our Earth became apparent when she was still very young. Her studies led her to landscape design and ecology. Today she is a fine botanist and agriculturist. She hopes to focus her energies to teach all children a healthy respect for the Earth and its bounty, to prevent further deterioration, and to restore what has been damaged—in other words, to be good stewards of the Earth and to enhance rather than diminish its resources.

Livia commutes to the Ranch from her home in England where her husband is completing his studies, and is responsible for our overall building and garden design.

This text would be incomplete without a tribute to Mexico, the land that welcomed us long ago. Our staff has been enriched by its hard-working, delightful people, who so well understand and practice the art of friendship.

Special recognition is due our general manager, José Manuel Jasso. A second-generation employee, he grew up on the Ranch and was a mere youngster when he first worked for us during summer vacations. His total dedication quickly advanced him to a position of authority and has earned him a full partnership in Rancho La Puerta with Alex and Livia Szekely.

Deborah, Alex and Livia Szekely

Our guests, too, have played a key role in our story. Extraordinary data verifying our capacity business extend back many years and confirm the Ranch guests' happy habit of returning again and again. They have kept us from preoccupation with such mundane matters as how to fill up room accommodations, and freed us to keep an eye on the future, with its vast potential for assisting our guests to achieve rare harmony with body, mind, and spirit.

Deborah Szekely

The New Nutrition
(Ours for Half a Century)

There is no fitness resort predating Rancho La Puerta.
And there is none so new.
During the many years when Rancho La Puerta and the Golden Door were propounding theories and then demonstrating and empirically proving them, we were one of the few sources for popular knowledge about what was going on in the field of natural health and preventive medicine.

How the situation has reversed. Avid for health news and too hopeful for miracles, today's press often practices overkill.

The Lesson of the Big Oat-Bran Rhubarb

Besides a rapid climb that brought it from far behind to midway on vegetable popularity charts, skyrocketing broccoli had just received journalistic acclaim for ability to help detoxify cancer, when came a put-down from Johns Hopkins Medical Institutions: To perform as a cancer detox, the broccoli in your supermarket may not have been kept fresh enough; the broccoli in your freezer may not have been frozen soon enough; just-plucked-from-the-garden-row broccoli, however, might be able to cut it*; but who knows? And who knows how much broccoli would be required to help nullify cancer cells?

Garlic has just grabbed the spotlight reserved for possible cancer deterrents. Folklore has long attributed amazing abilities to this member of the lily family. I believe they are true. But too extensive media coverage too much and too soon invites disappointment.

Here we have broccoli and garlic, two wonderfully worthwhile friends from the garden patch, in danger of sharing the fate of oat bran: discredit because they didn't succeed as nutritional superstars.

*Edmond Szekely always theorized that the most nutritiously effective food is that grown locally, processed as little as feasible and promptly eaten as near as possible to the point of origin. Both Rancho La Puerta and the Golden Door honor his precept closely by raising much of their own foodstuffs. (In the U.S., food averages a 1,300-mile trip from conception to consumption.) These facts may inspire you to plant your own garden patch. A supply of the freshest of vegetables and herbs will revivify your standby recipes and boost your own good health.

Broccoli remains a supervegetable.

Garlic is an indispensable flavoring. That it has a salutary effect upon the blood may yet be proven true.

Oat bran doesn't have to promise to lower our cholesterol count in order to deserve a place on the Ranch bill of fare. For 50 years we have preferred the Scottish Filed Oats variety, with all fibre intact.

How difficult it is – more so every day as science rivets its attention on nutrition – for the public to remain accurately informed.

For that reason we are including this overview of the why and what and how of Rancho La Puerta's recipes and menus.

How Sweet It Is

We have always avoided refined sugar and bleached white flour. Our sweetener of choice has consistently been completely natural wild-sage honey. For the first 30 years we gathered it from hives maintained on one of our ranches.

Honey is sweeter than sugar; therefore, less of it will do. At present this country produces about a hundred different flavors. They can bring brilliant variety to some of your everyday standby recipes. Their possible combinations are like the strains of a symphony when compared to the one repetitious note of refined sugar.

As for sugar substitutes, the Ranch and the "Door" eschew them all. We will not be embarrassed when, in time, such substitutes may be condemned or prohibited. However, you need not back off from occasionally tasting a substitute. Only long-time ingestion could be dangerous.

Let others offer themselves as sacrificial lambs for newly introduced substitutes for real food. Why should you take such a risk? Remember how often our Food and Drug Administration has reversed its own decisions and has had to recall products. Then reflect that honey, safely enjoyed for thousands of years, has even survived in ancient tombs.

Cold Turkey Is a Diet No-No

If your problem is that you're a sugar-abuser, be patient with yourself. The American reliance upon both sugar and salt is nothing but a habit. Some habits are more stubborn than others.

If you have not already – or at least not completely – converted to the Rancho La Puerta plan for eating to enliven your life, don't now take a sudden headlong plunge. Don't require yourself to abandon at once all your mealtime favorites or occasional indulgences. Recognize your dependence at present and for some time to come upon certain comfort foods. Introduce only gradual changes that are painless.

Step one is to begin serving yourself not too perceptibly smaller portions. Decalorize with such trusty stand-ins as honey instead of sugar; low-fat yogurt instead of sour cream; use of the broiler or a wok or simple poaching rather than the skillet; or a household rule that, if you haven't a nonstick pan to cook it in, you'll bake it.

Attack your sugar abuse imaginatively. With so many sparkling waters domestic and imported (check that they're low-sodium) on sale, surely one will please you as much as a soft drink. Top your glass with a lemon twist. Or put fresh fruit in the bottom.

Have you combined a herb tea with fresh fruit juice, half and half? Interesting and refreshing, and my own favorite for the past 30 years.

My late husband, a European gourmet despite his advanced theories on nutrition, was the first person I ever knew to freeze grapes for snacking. Now frozen grapes and frozen sliced bananas are popular between-meal snacks, permissible on any sensible diet. So is the instant ice cream you can process in a Champion Juicer (see Frozen Fruit Sorbet, page 95).

Never cheat yourself of your well-deserved low-calorie dessert as crown for a well-balanced meal. To do so may set you to dreaming about forbidden foods. (If your craving for some toothsome but taboo treat becomes overwhelming, satisfy it with just one big scrumptious bite.)

Proceed slowly. Set modest, reasonable goals. Reward yourself (never with food) whenever you achieve one of them.

Kicking the sugar habit can be a long process but need not be an unpleasant one. Don't think of it as deprivation. Realize that you are creating a more subtle and adult palate.

Effecting a Saline Solution

How often have you heard someone claim it would be impossible for her/him to give up salt? What nonsense. We know that in olden times salt was a delicacy which many people managed to do without very well. Perhaps that's how salt established such a hold on eating habits. The status-symbol aura must have hung on, an In fad that through the centuries unaccountably escaped any Out list. How else to explain people who senselessly sprinkle salt on a meal before tasting it?

Salt ranks high on the list of suspects as a contributor to high blood pressure. The human body needs less than a teaspoon of salt daily. If you eat canned, frozen or packaged foods, you may be unknowingly filling your quota before you have a chance to pick up your saltshaker. Salt and sugar head the ingredients most apt to be hidden in prepared foods. Their appearance in the fine print of a contents list may be disguised by a name not familiar to the average shopper. Sometimes on one label a manufacturer lists several aliases for salt or sugar. This can confuse you about the amount therein contained.

A lot of salt can also be secretly lurking in your city water supply.

Use of salt is such a totally acquired eating habit that it's fairly simple to correct permanently. If you gradually cut down on salt and then do without it for a period of time, your desire for that salty taste will be gone. Vanished. With no problems of backsliding.

Here's a secret from ex-Golden Door nutritionist Sheri Lee Shansby (quoted in the *New York Times*): Combine citrus juice and chervil to give a recipe a taste of salt.

3

You can easily banish salt from most of your regular recipes. At first you may want to add salt just before eating but as you experiment with alternate seasonings you'll eventually be able to sweep the offending shaker off your table for good. By then, you will have refined and expanded your seasoning preferences. In place of humdrum salt you'll be savoring a world of herbs and spices.

A Freshet of Freshness

If you're from a generation who saw mostly carrot-and-pea side dishes and lettuce-and-tomato salads routed your way in a monotonous parade from the kitchen, and were committed to eating them because you were assured that they were good for you, you're rejoicing over the new flamboyance of American produce. Root and cruciferous vegetables, exotic mushrooms, ruffly lettuces, fresh herbs with a sassy way with them (so superior to the dried and pre-packaged) — all in such profusion of varieties that a greengrocer's today can be as pretty as a florist's.

It's no hardship to select 4 or more daily servings of fresh vegetables, just because they are so appealing. Eat a certain number of them raw. Don't overcook the rest. Steaming is ideal. It leaves potassium and other great minerals and vitamins intact. Light stir-frying is an option too.

After you've concocted an enticing salad, you want a dressing worthy of it — something that will respect the independence of all the deftly assembled tastes and textures and yet make a notable contribution of its own. You will wish to mix it yourself.

Among oils, the classic contribution to salads is that of the olive. In the revised edition of my *Secrets of the Golden Door* (Bantam paperback, 1979), I appended a new recipe section in which olive oil was my consistent choice for salads. My rationale in 1979 was that a fine salad and the finest of oils deserve each other — and our low-calorie recipes used such minute quantities of olive oil that they were surely beyond reproach. Disclosure that olive oil, so high in monounsaturated fat, may outperform vegetable oils in reducing blood cholesterol, has now caused a rush on this Italian import.

The F Word

Like canola (formerly rapeseed), avocado, almond and peanut oils, olive belongs to the elite fat group called monounsaturated. Canola oil earns points for being highest in monounsaturates and lowest in saturates. Olive oil is not far behind in terms of desirable percentages and popularity.*

The Numero Segundo good-guy fat group, polyunsaturated, embraces corn, walnut, sesame, sunflower and safflower oils; also, lean meats like skinless chicken and such seafoods as shrimp and sardines.

---

*True, olive oil's calorie and fat gram count check out higher than the data shown for butter and margarine. But butter is loaded with saturated animal fat. As for margarine, in Summer 1990 it inspired news squibs that invariably began, "Recently it has come to the attention of nutritionists…" and then proceeded to question even the conditional

Saturated (bad guy) fats are rife in dairy products and meats as well as in some oils of nonanimal origin. The worst of these, because of the overwhelming presence of evil lauric acid, are palm kernel and coconut oil, until only a while ago injected willy-nilly into processed foods till manufacturers were shamed into replacing them.

Nevertheless, it seems that even a saturated fat has a place in Nature's plan. Latest nutritional advice suggests that you trisect your day's fats intake among the three types, with emphasis of course on mono- and polyunsaturates.

Instructions for determining your daily fat quota have been distributed widely. You perhaps remember the formula: Write down your total daily calories. Divide the figure by 30 (that's the maximum percentage of your calories that should derive from fats — less than 30 would be more ideal). The resultant number represents your total permissible daily fat grams.

Fat is causing a furor.

The chief problem with fat is its relation to cholesterol and hardening of the arteries.

There is the cholesterol which enters the body through animal foods we eat, the cholesterol which the body itself manufactures — and then the accumulation of body cholesterol which increases with time, so that the cholesterol deposits at the end of a long life may work against one's enjoying a healthy old age.

Cholesterol is a complex subject, made more so by exploratory studies which from time to time bring us revelations on the subject or tend to contradict previous beliefs.

With Egg on Their Faces

Experts who make these important calculations have lately admitted that eggs — like shrimp (not so long ago) — are innocent of excessive cholesterol. (Total for an average large egg: 213 mg, not 274.)

Even without this go-ahead, it was a likely bet that, if you have been a vegetarian for a number of years and have normal low cholesterol as so many vegetarians do, you could safely eat as many as two eggs a day, three or four times a week. Meat-eaters should first learn their cholesterol count; if a problem exists, when their cholesterol level is brought down they too can eat eggs once or twice weekly.

But you must also take into account your hereditary influences. High cholesterol seems to be part of some families' patterns. There are certain people who should consume eggs only infrequently — and should eat only half as much egg yolk as egg white.

Whole Protein

It is official that excess protein can harm the kidneys — excess mean-

---

approval for margarine soft enough to be sold in small tubs. In November 1990 the *Mayo Clinic Newsletter* took a pro-margarine poke at butter. The butter-margarine controversy has been and will remain a long one. (My own preference is butter because it's a more natural product. I use it so sparingly it cannot possibly pose a problem.)

ing anything above 10-15 percent of your daily caloric intake.

Today, in an effort to make beef lower in calories and cholesterol and higher in sales, the meat industry is trimming most of that visible fat which we didn't want anyway but always had to pay for. In addition, cattlemen are breeding for more leanness.

The U.S. beef industry has other problems to solve: The European Community has boycotted all imports of America's hormone-injected meat. The U.S. defense was that nobody ever died from such beef. But it would seem that it should be anyone's prerogative to boycott food injected with hormones or any other extraneous substance.

Luckily, health-food stores can usually put you in touch with chickens that have not been puffed up with hormone shots. Pristine beef, however, isn't so easy to come by.

Some (nonvegetarian) food experts are recommending that a sizeable part of your daily protein intake be nonanimal in origin.

One nutritionist offers this handy rule of thumb: At any meal, plant foods should cover 3/4 of your plate, and seafood or meat or dairy foods should occupy the remainder.

And What About Piscine Protein?

Several years ago Rancho La Puerta modified its lacto-ovo-vegetarian menu with the introduction of twice-weekly fish – a logical decision, since the beautiful waters off Baja California still possess one of the world's outstanding natural fish traps.

Other waters have not fared so well. The penchant for dumping has caused widespread seafood contamination.

At presstime the federal government is addressing itself to this problem and answering to criticism of lax inspection of our food fish.

The world has permitted most coastal waters and freshwater rivers to become polluted. Avoid their fish and shellfish. Rely on fish from the open ocean. Or purchase trout from carefully controlled fish farms. And remember that fish – like chicken – should be trimmed of skin and fat.

Complex Carbohydrates

Only a few years ago, complex carbohydrates were not a well-recognized classification. Recently we have been officially advised to derive 60 percent of our daily calories from them.

Since then, cooking labs have been scrambling to devise new ways to prepare legumes, pasta, potatoes, seeds, whole grains and complex-carbo vegetables. Rancho La Puerta stole a half-century march on anyone else. Our vegetarian principles always dictated that complex carbohydrates be the basis of our guests' diet.

I trust that you play by the rules and do not smother pasta in cheese and other high-fat ingredients, or serve the common bleached white-flour variety of pasta, so protein-poor. Look to whole-wheat or vegetable pasta for worthwhile nutritional value.

Way back in 1971 farsighted author Frances Moore Lappé wrote *Diet for a Small Planet*. It's still available in paperback from Bantam, and gives clear, comprehensive instructions for combining complex carbos into complete proteins. Do acquire it.

One of the most durable paperbacks in publishing history, Lappé's little book has sold 3 million copies. She herself is now universally recognized as an expert on relieving world hunger.

Fibre

If you treat yourself to 4 or more servings a day from the Vegetable-Fruit Group and the same amount from the Bread-Cereal Group, as well as a good representation from other Complex Carbohydrates, you'll surely eat sufficient fibre.

Water Rights

Next to air, water is the food your body consumes in greatest quantity. You need 6-8 glasses of water daily. You deserve as pure as can be found — even if it means installing a water-purification system, or buying bottled (low-sodium) water.

Vitamins and Minerals

Personally, I always shop at health-food stores for normal-strength vitamin and mineral supplements made of natural substances. It has been rightly said that a correct diet precludes any need for such pills. But who can guarantee a perfect diet? A daily supply of one nutrient can even be inadvertently nullified if combined with another nutrient. Soil and weather conditions and time of harvesting can cause vitamin and mineral content to differ vastly from the expected. Some food substances that are nutrient-rich when they leave the farm may reach the consumer in weakened condition because freshness is so crucial a factor. Vitamins and minerals are literally leaking all over your fridge, as they did in the produce section and, before that, in the vehicle which transported them.

I think supplements are often necessary, particularly for people who try to balance a sedentary life by eating very lightly.

Skipped Meals and Other Capital Offenses

When you skip a meal — or any time you let yourself become too hungry — you set yourself up for gorging.

One of the tragedies of failed diet attempts is that so many people imagine one big violation of the diet plan automatically compels them to lose their next turn and proceed back to Start. Not wishing to begin all over again, they abort their mission. Quit. Give up until the next diet-of-the-month comes by.

It is now generally accepted that a dietary seesaw is bad for one both physically and psychologically. You demand a great deal of hard work from your body every time you gain and lose weight. Gain-lose, gain-lose over the years and your body, tiring of this nonsense, can begin to slow down your response to dieting.

Get off the seesaw. Stop looking for no-calorie pie-in-the-sky. If a weight-loss diet sounds unbelievably easy, don't pin any hopes to it.

Once off the seesaw, find your balance. Don't think in terms of temporary diets at all. Tell yourself you are going to take a sensible new direction. It will not be stressful. You are going to establish an entirely different way of eating and of moving through your world. Its results will be permanent because you will concentrate only on ways to bring about permanent change. You will progress very slowly. You will set the simplest of diet and exercise goals, reward yourself when you achieve them, and never never punish yourself (or give up) if you slip or take a backward step. This is a lifetime matter—you needn't hurry.

How to Psych Yourself into Better Eating Habits

I have looked about for some little up-to-the-minute hints that can be simply practiced to great effect. But I find mostly repetition of the advice I myself have been disseminating for years:

Start by regarding your new plan as the grand design it is. But begin with the most elementary minor changes. Look over your own kitchen file and decide which recipes you can decalorize by making do with ⅓ to ½ less sugar and/or ¼ less oil or fat. Reduce servings by 1/4. Enhance them by placing your lunch or dinner on a salad plate.

Why not use your best china? If you are eating alone, do it in style. Set your meal on a tray. Flatter yourself with the gift of a single rose. Carry your tray to the most appealing outdoor or indoor setting that is convenient. Eat slowly (chewy food is best). Allow nothing to interfere with your thoughts of and pleasure in what you are eating.

If you have a meal partner, make sure that all serving is done from the kitchen so you won't be tempted by the proximity of seconds.

Don't leave yourself open to seduction by prohibited snacks. Stock plenty of legitimate ones, such as air-popped, unsalted, herb-seasoned unbuttered popcorn, vegetable sticks and luscious fresh fruit.

Yes, Label Reading Can Be Laborious, But—

In 1990, 93 percent of all shoppers (according to survey) felt genuine concern about the contents of food purveyed in U.S. markets. About 40 percent were so concerned that they habitually read food-product labels, with particular attention to fat, salt and calories. Only 8 percent of us never read a label at all.

---

*As a board member of the Center for Science in the Public Interest, it's my pleasure to advise you that CSPI puts out one of the most enlightening and fascinating newsletters, bar none. *Nutrition Action Healthletter* is published 10 times annually and is available by

The statistics are admirable but the results sometimes frustrating in view of the amount of mystery that can be crowded onto just one food label. We can only hope that the reformed guidelines of our Secretary of Health and Human Services will clarify the situation soon.

Meantime, those of you who carry reading glasses and pocket calculator to the supermarket should continue your careful monitoring. To help you identify some of the obscure ingredient names you encounter, let me suggest a kitchen poster you can check just before your shopping forays. Called "Chemical Cuisine" and copyright 1989, it is distributed by the Center for Science in the Public Interest, 1875 Connecticut Avenue, N.W., Suite 300, Washington, D.C. 20009-5728.

If all this sounds like a good deal of work, consider an easy healthy alternative: Cut back on processed foods, and read so much less fine-print gobbledygook.*

Prognosis Positive

What are we to make of the quantities of puzzling data I find in my current clipping file for General Nutrition, Health and Fitness? Just as we start to rejoice over some hopeful development, a conflicting report seems to shoot it down...

Since 1979 a company called Nutriguide evaluates and tickets more than 2,000 grocery items; many stores now subscribe to this service ... Ralphs Grocery Company has just instituted a new-product identification program ... In many cities you can go on supermarket tours led by savvy guides with eye-opening information ... One supermarket chain experimented with a sugarless aisle ... Although Americans eat more fresh produce, they are grossing out on more and more sweets ... Yet the quality of the produce section is the criterion by which most shoppers choose a supermarket ... Despite concern about fats, mayo-spreads-salad dressings are a billion-dollar market ... Take-out food orders are soaring, with pizzas blasting off every second ... While claiming that they enjoy cooking, a vast percentage of singles never do any, depriving themselves of one of life's primal sensuous pleasures: food handling ... An aggressive and progressive alliance for diet reform is the new league of professional chefs and nutritionists ... A Gallup Poll survey of family-dining habits disclosed that, in a typical week, only 25 percent ate as many as 7 prepared-from-scratch meals of fresh ingredients ... This country, once locked into a rigid steak-and-potatoes cuisine mentality, is growing adventurous; witness the surprising proliferation of ethnic restaurants large and small ... In 1977, fats hogged 40 percent of the U.S. diet. The figure has dropped to 37 percent – not ideal but promising ... Inno-

---

subscription only from the Center. Also available from CSPI is a striking and useful series of kitchen posters. Particularly recommended: "Nutrition Scoreboard."
For more information, write or call (202) 332-9110.

vators are seeking such breakthroughs as much lower-calorie cheeses—
and fresh fruits small enough for vending machines ... An expert al-
leges that surveyed Americans perceive themselves as nutritionally much
more straight-arrow than they in fact are, and that polls often reflect
mere lip service to good nutrition ... Another expert complains that
too many Americans wishfully believe in the big nutrition fix, the one
impossible miracle food that will be the ultimate cure-all ...

This is a bulky file from which I've been quoting. It indicates the
tremendous energy now being channeled into goals of better health and
better living. It suggests the vigor with which Americans have responded
to the New Fitness and the New Nutrition. It promises that we will
never again slip into complacency with an unsatisfactory status quo.

Living Younger Longer

A diet plan must pair with an exercise plan to be successful. Once
you are in gear, use these recipes in tandem with sensible exercise.

Quality food alone will not assure quality life.

Don't equate the importance of regular exercise with the limited space
allotted it in this chapter of a book dealing with food. (I already have
an all-exercise book seeking a publisher.)

As essential as the basic food groups* are to your daily nutrition, so
is the hour of exercise which your body requires each day. Whether you
perform a full hour of consecutive movement or take several exercise
breaks is immaterial. Critical is the opting for an exercise menu as var-
ied as that of your salads: walking, swimming, aerobics, weight-training,
tennis, etc. You must find an agreeable practicable system for stretching
out and working out your entire body.

The old adage "Use it or lose it" was never more pertinent than when
applied to bodily movement. Not only bones, muscle and sinew are in-
volved. Arms and legs are the pump handles of the heart. It is possible
to survive for weeks without food, days without water—but within mo-
ments after the oxygen supply stops, the body dies.

Movement provides the breath of life.

A fit person of 70 can surpass an unfit person of 35 in the so-essential
transporting of oxygen (a primary indication of the body's vital function).

Fortunately, it is within our power to catch up, to mitigate the risk
factors of today's sedentary life-style.

Many of us now live into our 80s. This is the first time in history that
people have held the key to determining the quality of the final third
of their own lives. You alone can choose what these years will be: re-
warding, joyous or quite miserable.

Your body is the tool with which you shape your life. Only good nutrition and good exercise habits will keep that tool well honed, effective
and able to respond to your every need.

*Children should learn them at the same time as the 3 primary colors. You probably don't
need to be reminded of the food groups but I'd like to tell you how I prefer to break them
down, reserving a special classification for complex carbos; next come grains and breads;
beans, nuts and seeds; meat, poultry and dairy products (including cultures such as yogurt and acidophilus); seafood; fresh fruits and vegetables; and a please-take-it-easy but
indispensable subgroup: condiments.

Favorite Recipes

The following recipes are based upon an average intake of 1,000 daily calories.

Rancho La Puerta allots its guests approximately 250-300 calories for breakfast, 300 for luncheon and 400-450 for dinner.

Breakfast at the Ranch usually brings out a selection of fresh ripe fruits such as papaya, banana or berries; cereal, hot high-fibre (such as steel-cut oats with cinnamon, raisins and 2%-fat milk) or cold, unsweetened; for those who don't have elevated cholesterol levels, fresh eggs or low-fat yogurt and choice of a moist wheat-bran/oat-bran muffin or a toasted slice of our famous whole-wheat bread.

Luncheon means a light soup and a luncheon salad. Or a luncheon entrée may be accompanied by a dinner salad. Dinner begins with a dinner salad or soup (both, if total calories don't exceed the dinner allowance). The dinner entrée follows. Dinner ends with the accent that only a delightful dessert can provide.

You'll find our recipes adapt smoothly for people who (probably like you and certainly like me) can schedule only limited time in the kitchen. All the salad dressings and sauces can be made in advance and frozen. Quick-cooking grains such as bulgur wheat, couscous and Basmati rice can be substituted for long-cooking grains. Black and kidney beans can take over for long-cooking legumes. You can prepare these in large quantities and store in your freezer. But if kept on ice more than 3 months, their nutritional value and flavor will dissipate.

Some statistician has estimated that there are now 17,000 weight-loss systems. Aren't you relieved that Rancho La Puerta long ago investigated the foremost among them, so that you won't have to? Our amazingly effective plan we don't think of as a diet at all (and neither should you). It's a total program for building a lifetime of buoyant good health, and it works so well that it has brought us hundreds of thousands of guests, many of whom are motivated to return again and again.

Black bean soup with cumin and tomatoes.

Soups

Black-Bean Soup with Cumin and Tomatoes

½ cup	dried black-beans, rinsed and sorted
1 tsp	canola or olive oil*
1	medium onion, quartered
1	carrot, chopped
1	bay leaf
4 cups	White Vegetable Stock (page 18)
½ lb	tomatoes, chopped
¼ lb	green bell peppers, seeded and diced
1	celery stalk, diced
2	green onions, diced
2	garlic cloves, minced
1	small jalapeño chile,** minced (or ¼ tsp dried chili flakes)
1 Tbsp	ground cumin
2 tsp	fresh oregano, chopped
1	bay leaf
2 Tbsp	fresh cilantro, chopped
	black pepper, freshly ground, to taste
6 Tbsp	non-fat plain yogurt

In large bowl cover beans with water by 4″. Refrigerate overnight; drain. Sauté onion and carrot with bay leaf until onion is golden; set aside. Bring Stock to boil in large pot. Stir in beans; cook, covered, over medium-low heat 40 minutes. Purée 1½ cups bean-Stock mixture. Return to pot; stir in remaining ingredients except cilantro and yogurt. Simmer, covered, 45 minutes. Remove cover, stir in cilantro, cook 20 minutes more. Remove bay leaf. Season. Ladle into soup bowls; top each with 1 Tbsp yogurt.

Makes 6 ⅔-cup servings of 116 calories each.

*Non-stick vegetable spray may be used to lightly coat the pan.

**See note page 101.

Carrot Bisque with Curry

During winter, substitute butternut or pumpkin squash for carrots.

1 tsp	canola or olive oil*
1 lb	carrots, peeled and cut in ¼" slices
1 cup	onion, chopped
2 tsp	fresh ginger, peeled and minced
2 tsp	curry powder
1	garlic clove, minced
4 cups	White Vegetable Stock (page 18)
large pinch	white pepper
4 tsp	fresh mint, chopped (garnish)
4 tsp	sunflower seeds (optional for garnish)

Sauté onion and carrots in oil until onion is golden. Add curry, ginger and garlic; cook 5 minutes over medium heat. Transfer vegetables to medium pot and combine with Stock. Bring to boil; reduce heat. Simmer, covered, 40-45 minutes, or until carrots are very tender. Remove from heat and process in blender or food processor until smooth. Return soup to pot; season with pepper. Reheat over low heat. Ladle into 4 bowls. Garnish each with 1 tsp mint and 1 tsp sunflower seeds (optional).

Makes about 4 ⅔-cup servings of 289 calories each.

*Non-stick vegetable spray may be used to lightly coat the pan.

Chilled Melon Soup

1	small honeydew, cut into 1" cubes
½ cup	fresh orange juice
¼ cup plus 3 Tbsp	non-fat plain yogurt
1 tsp	fresh lime juice
½ tsp	fresh tarragon, minced (or ¼ tsp dried)
pinch	ground nutmeg
	lime zest,* minced (garnish)

In food processor combine melon, juices, ¼ cup yogurt, tarragon and nutmeg. Purée until smooth, about 2 minutes. Pour into bowl. Refrigerate, covered, at least 2 hours, until chilled.

Divide among 4 small bowls. Divide remaining yogurt on top each portion. Garnish and serve.

Makes 4 servings of 88 calories each.

*See note page 102.

Chunky Gazpacho with Cucumber

¾ cup	Piquant Ranch Salsa* (page 34)
1 cup	low-sodium V8 vegetable juice
¼ cup	celery, diced
⅓ cup	cucumber, peeled, seeded and finely diced
¼ cup	red onion, diced
8-10 drops	Tabasco sauce, or to taste
⅛ tsp	black pepper, freshly ground
	leafy celery stalks (garnish)

Combine all ingredients. Chill a few hours before serving, so flavors blend and mellow. Pour into very chilled bowls or stem glasses. Garnish.

Makes about 4 ⅔-cup servings of 28 calories each.

*Substitute 1 Tbsp fresh oregano (or ½ tsp dried leaves) for cilantro in salsa recipe.

Hearty Yellow Split-Pea Soup

¾ cup	yellow split peas (or ½ cup green split peas), rinsed and sorted
1	onion, quartered
4 cups	White Vegetable Stock (page 18) or water
large pinch	cayenne pepper
1 tsp	canola or olive oil*
1	large carrot (¼ lb), peeled and diced
2	celery ribs, diced
1	large onion, chopped
1	bay leaf
2	garlic cloves, minced
2 tsp	fresh oregano, chopped (or ⅛ tsp dried leaves)
4	fresh thyme sprigs (or ½ tsp dried leaves)
	black pepper, freshly ground, to taste

In large bowl, cover peas with water by 4". Refrigerate overnight; drain. In large pot combine quartered onion, peas, cayenne pepper and Stock; simmer, covered, 1 hour.

Sauté carrot, celery, chopped onion, bay leaf, garlic and herbs in 1 tsp oil until onion is golden. Purée 1 cup peas-Stock mixture and return to pot. Add sautéed vegetables to simmered peas; remove bay leaf and cook 15-20 additional minutes over low heat until peas are completely soft. Adjust seasonings, with freshly ground pepper to taste.

Makes about 4 1-cup servings of 90 calories each.

*Non-stick vegetable spray may be used to lightly coat the pan.

Lentil Soup with Swiss Chard and Thyme

1 tsp canola or olive oil*
1 medium onion, chopped
1 small leek, halved lengthwise, with half of green part removed, cleaned and chopped
2 garlic cloves, minced
1 medium carrot, peeled and diced
1 celery rib, diced
1 Tbsp fresh sage, chopped (or 1 tsp dried leaves)
1 Tbsp fresh thyme, chopped (or 1 tsp dried leaves)
1 bay leaf
1 small boiling potato, peeled and diced
⅓ cup dried lentils
4 cups White Vegetable Stock (page 18)
½ lb tomatoes, chopped
1 medium zucchini, diced
¼ lb Swiss chard, ribs removed and shredded
2 Tbsp fresh parsley, chopped
1 tsp low-sodium soy sauce*
¼ tsp black pepper, freshly ground

In large pot sauté onion, leek, garlic, carrot, celery and herbs until onion is golden; set aside. Simmer lentils and potato with Stock 40-45 minutes (lentils and potato should be cooked but firm). Add Stock mixture to onion-carrot sauté along with tomatoes, zucchini and chard. Bring to boil, covered over medium heat and simmer 15-20 minutes. Stir in parsley, soy sauce and pepper. Simmer, uncovered, 10 minutes more.

Makes 6 1-cup servings of 71 calories each.

*Non-stick vegetable spray may be used to lightly coat the pot.

**See note page 102.

Potato-Leek Soup with Fresh Sage

4½ cups   White Vegetable Stock (page 18)
½ lb   leeks, white parts only, halved lengthwise, cleaned and chopped
1   garlic clove, minced
1   bay leaf
⅓ tsp   fresh sage, chopped (or ½ tsp dried leaves)
1 lb   boiling potatoes, peeled and diced
          white pepper and ground nutmeg, to taste
2 Tbsp   chives, chopped (garnish)

In large pot combine ½ cup Stock, leeks, garlic, sage and bay leaf. Cook, covered, over low heat 10 minutes or until leeks are very soft. Add remaining Stock, bring to boil and stir in potatoes. Cook, covered, over medium-low heat, 20 minutes, or until potatoes are very tender. Remove bay leaf. Purée soup in 2 batches. Return soup to pot. Season. Reheat over low heat. Ladle soup into 6 bowls; garnish each with 1 tsp chives.

Makes 6 ¾-cup servings of 94 calories each.

White Vegetable Stock

1   large leek, halved lengthwise, with half of green part removed, cleaned
3   baking potatoes, unpeeled
6   carrots, peeled
8   celery stalks
3   medium zucchini
2   large unpeeled onions, quartered
½ lb   fresh mushrooms, quartered
1 head   unpeeled garlic, cloves crushed
10   black peppercorns
8   fresh thyme sprigs
8   fresh parsley sprigs
3   bay leaves

Cut leek, potatoes, carrots, celery and zucchini in 1″ pieces.

In large stock pot combine all ingredients; cover with water by 6″. Bring to boil; reduce heat and simmer, covered, 1 hour. Skim top if necessary.

Remove cover; simmer 45 minutes or until stock is flavorful. Strain, pressing against vegetables to extract as much flavor and stock as possible.

Makes about 8 cups (calories negligible).

Stock can be refrigerated up to 4 days, or frozen up to 4 months.

Winter Squash Soup

1 tsp	canola or olive oil*			
1	small onion, diced	1½ tsp	fresh ginger, minced
1 cup	celery, diced	1 tsp	ground nutmeg
½ cup	carrots, diced	¼ tsp	fresh thyme
½ lb	butternut or Hubbard squash, peeled, cut in 1″ pcs	¼ tsp	white pepper
		1 qt	White Vegetable Stock (page 18)

Sauté onion, celery and carrot in medium pot over medium heat until onion is golden; add squash and cook 5 more minutes. Add Stock and seasonings; simmer over low heat 30 minutes or until squash is soft and breaks apart with fork. Cool slightly. Purée soup (in two batches) in blender or food processor until smooth.

Makes 6 servings of 49 calories each.

*Non-stick vegetable spray may be used to lightly coat the pot.

Tempeh tostada salad with tomatillo salsa.

Salads

Cabbage Salad with Bleu Cheese, Apples and Walnuts

½ lb	red cabbage
½ lb	green or Chinese cabbage
1	large red apple, grated
1	large green onion, chopped
4 tsp	bleu cheese (¼ oz), crumbled
4 tsp	walnuts, toasted, chopped
	black pepper, freshly ground, to taste
1	large shallot
¼ cup	water
¼ cup	apple-cider or pear vinegar
¼ cup	unsweetened apple juice
1 Tbsp	extra virgin olive oil* or walnut oil
2 tsp	Dijon-type mustard*
¼ tsp	caraway seed

Remove 6 medium-size leaves from red cabbage; reserve. Quarter remaining cabbage and shred lengthwise. In large bowl toss shredded cabbage, apple, onion, cheese and walnuts.

In food processor or blender mix all remaining ingredients (except pepper) until smooth. In small pan heat mix; boil 1 minute. Pour this vinaigrette mix over cabbage mix. Toss well. Chill 1 hour, stirring occasionally. Season with pepper. Put reserved red cabbage leaf on each of 6 salad plates. Top with about 1 cup cabbage salad. Serve chilled.

Makes 6 servings of 95 calories each.

*See note page 101.

Cucumber and Red Onion Salad with Fresh Dill

		2 Tbsp	fresh lemon juice
		2 tsp	white wine vinegar
		2 tsp	fresh dill, minced
		1 tsp	extra virgin olive oil*
			black pepper, freshly ground, to taste
1	large English or domestic cucumber (½ lb)	4	large lettuce leaves, rinsed, spun dry
2 Tbsp	red onion, chopped	4	fresh dill sprigs (garnish)

If skin is waxed, peel cucumber. Cut lengthwise, scoop out seeds. Dice into ¼" pcs. In medium bowl stir cucumber with onion, lemon juice, vinegar, dill and oil. Season with pepper. Chill 1 hour.

Put lettuce leaf on each of 4 salad plates. Divide cucumber mix onto each. Garnish. Serve chilled.

Makes 4 servings of 32 calories each.

*See note page 101.

Garden Harvest Salad

		½ lb	asparagus, trimmed
		2	medium zucchini, cut in 1" slices
2 cups	medium broccoli florets	¼ lb	snow peas, trimmed
2 cups	medium cauliflower florets	2	yellow squash, cut in 1" slices
2	large carrots, cut in ½" slices	2 cups	low-fat cottage cheese
		2	lemons, halved

Steam vegetables individually until just tender but crisp; chill. Divide vegetables, cottage cheese and lemons onto 4 plates.

Makes 4 servings of 188 calories each.

Seasonal Fresh Fruit Salad

Crown with Vanilla-Yogurt (page 99) and Strawberry (page 98) Sauces.

2 cups	whole fresh strawberries (1 pt)
2 cups	melon, peeled, diced in 1″ pcs
1	small papaya or mango, peeled, cut in 1″ pcs
1⅓ cups	pineapple, peeled, diced in 1″ pcs
1 cup	fresh raspberries, blackberries or blueberries
2	medium peaches, nectarines or plums, pitted, cut in ½″ slices
2 cups	low-fat plain yogurt
	fresh mint sprigs (garnish – optional)

Divide fruit onto 4 plates. Garnish if desired. Serve chilled.
Makes 4 servings of 178 calories each.

Winter Variation

Substitute summer fruits with 2 cups each, diced grapefruit and orange sections; 1 red or green medium apple, cored, cut in 1″ pcs; 1⅓ cups pear, cut in 1″ pcs; 1 cup frozen unsweetened raspberries, blackberries or blueberries (thawed); 1 medium banana, peeled, cut in ½″ pcs.

Spinach and Goat-Cheese Salad with Balsamic Vinaigrette

2 large bunches	spinach leaves, rinsed, spun dry, tightly packed in 4 cups
½ small head	radicchio (about 1½ oz), cut in thin strips
¼ cup	Balsamic Vinaigrette (page 31)
1 oz	mild goat cheese or fresh feta, crumbled
	black pepper, freshly ground, to taste

Stack 12 spinach leaves at a time, roll up and cut in ½″-thick strips to make a chiffonade. In large bowl toss radicchio and spinach chiffonade with Vinaigrette. Divide onto 4 plates. Sprinkle with cheese. Season with pepper. Serve chilled.

Makes 4 servings of 71 calories each.

24

Tempeh Tostada Salad with Tomatillo Salsa

	nonstick vegetable spray
½	white onion, chopped
6 oz	tempeh, chopped
2 tsp	ground cumin
1 tsp	chili powder
1	red bell pepper
1	yellow bell pepper
4-5	garlic cloves, minced
1	jalapeño pepper,* seeded and minced

1 Tbsp	ground cumin, or to taste
1 Tbsp	chili powder, or to taste
1	large red or yellow tomato
1	large bunch cilantro
	romaine lettuce, shredded
1	large red tomato, wedged
1	large yellow tomato, wedged
2 oz	jalapeño-soy cheese or low-sodium cheese, freshly grated
2	corn tortillas, cut into 16 wedges, baked crisp
½ cup	Tomatillo Salsa with Cilantro (page 34)

Heat medium pan and spray with nonstick vegetable spray. Cook onion until soft. Add tempeh and brown. Stir in cumin and chili powder. Set aside. Spray another pan; sauté bell peppers, garlic and jalapeño pepper until very soft; add remaining spices and tomato, and cook until tomato softens. Combine tempeh with vegetables; cook over low heat 2 minutes; add cilantro and remove from heat.

Line 4 plates with romaine. Evenly spoon tempeh in center of each plate. Arrange tomato wedges across lettuce and tempeh. Sprinkle cheese on salad edges. On each plate arrange 4 tortilla chips, and pour over 2 Tbsp Tomatillo Salsa.

Makes 4 servings of 264 calories each.

*See note page 101.

Watercress and Avocado Salad with Grapefruit Vinaigrette

1 medium bunch   butter lettuce, rinsed, spun dry

1 bunch   watercress, trimmed, rinsed, spun dry

1   grapefruit, peeled, pith removed with serrated knife; sectioned, skin and seeds removed

½   small avocado, peeled, cut in 8 slices

4 tsp   chives, chopped

¼ cup   Grapefruit Vinaigrette (page 33)

Divide greens onto 4 salad plates. Arrange about 2 grapefruit slices and 2 avocado slices on each plate. Sprinkle each with 1 tsp chives; add about 1 Tbsp Vinaigrette. Serve chilled.

Makes 4 servings of 100 calories each.

Dining Room—
Rancho La Puerta
1954

Avocado sauce with lemon and fresh herbs.

Salad Dressings & Sauces

Ancho Chile Sauce

2 large ancho* chiles (about 1½ oz)
2 cups low-sodium V8 vegetable juice
½ cup onion, coarsely chopped
2 large garlic cloves
1 large tomato, quartered
¼ tsp ground cumin
½ small jalapeño chile,* chopped (or ¼ tsp dried chili flakes)

Toast all vegetables over open flame or in a very hot, dry sauté pan until lightly charred (12-15 minutes). Remove seeds and stems from chiles.

In medium pot combine all ingredients. Bring to boil; simmer, covered, over low heat 20 minutes. Purée in blender or food processor until smooth.

Makes about 2 cups, or 8 ¼-cup servings of 30 calories each.

Covered, can be refrigerated up to 5 days; or frozen up to 3 months.

*See note page 101.

Avocado Sauce with Lemon and Fresh Herbs

Convert to a spicy guacamole sauce by addition of cilantro, chopped jalapeño* chile and/or ground cumin; serve with crispy baked tortilla wedges.

¾ cup non-fat plain yogurt
½ small avocado, peeled and seeded
1 large lemon, peeled, pith removed with serrated knife; skin and seeds removed
1 large garlic clove
2 tsp fresh dill, cilantro or basil, minced
black pepper, freshly ground, to taste

In food processor or blender process all ingredients (except fresh herb and black pepper) till smooth. Transfer to small bowl; stir in desired herb. Season.

Makes 1¼ cups, or 10 2-Tbsp servings of 25 calories each.

*See note page 101.

Balsamic Vinaigrette

This dressing adds pizzazz to fresh pasta.

1	large shallot
¼ cup	hot water
2 Tbsp	balsamic vinegar
1½ Tbsp	extra virgin olive oil* or walnut oil
1 Tbsp	fresh basil, chopped (or 1 tsp dried leaves)
	black pepper, freshly ground, to taste
1 Tbsp	bleu cheese, crumbled (¼ oz) (optional)

In food processor or blender combine all ingredients except cheese; process until smooth. If desired, stir cheese into dressing.

Makes about ½ cup, or 4 2-Tbsp servings of 75 calories each.

Can be refrigerated, covered, up to 5 days.

*See note page 101.

Creamy Ranch Dressing

½ cup	low-fat cottage cheese
⅓ cup	low-fat buttermilk
1 Tbsp	fresh lemon juice
1 Tbsp	Parmesan cheese, freshly grated
1	medium shallot
1	garlic clove
2 tsp	fresh basil, chopped (or ¼ tsp dried leaves)
½ tsp	fresh oregano, chopped (or ⅛ tsp dried leaves)
¼ tsp	fresh thyme, chopped (or ⅛ tsp dried leaves)
⅛ tsp	black pepper, freshly ground

Combine all ingredients in food processor or blender until smooth.

Makes about 1 cup, or 8 2-Tbsp servings of 25 calories each.

Can be refrigerated, covered, up to 4 days.

Fresh Herb-Mustard Vinaigrette

½ cup	fresh basil leaves, lightly packed
¼ cup	hot water or White Vegetable Stock (page 18)
2 Tbsp	white wine vinegar
1 Tbsp	extra virgin olive oil*
1	large lemon, peeled, pith removed with serrated knife; skin and seeds removed
1	medium shallot
2 tsp	Dijon-type mustard*
⅛ tsp	black pepper, freshly ground

In food processor or blender combine all ingredients until smooth.

Makes about ½ cup, or 6 2-Tbsp servings of 32 calories each.

Can be refrigerated, covered, up to 5 days.

*See note page 101.

Fresh Tomato-Basil Sauce

3½ lbs	tomatoes, chopped
1 cup	onion, chopped
5	garlic cloves, minced
6	fresh thyme sprigs (or 1 tsp dried thyme leaves)
1	bay leaf
¼ tsp	dried chili flakes
1 Tbsp	tomato paste, for color (optional)
	black pepper, freshly ground, to taste
¼ cup	fresh parsley
¼ cup	fresh basil, chopped (or 1 tsp dried basil, added as tomatoes cook)

In large non-aluminum pan combine all ingredients except tomato paste, parsley and fresh basil. Cook, uncovered, over medium heat 20-25 minutes or until tomatoes are soft and mix is thick. Remove bay leaf. Stir in tomato paste if desired. Season with pepper. Stir in fresh parsley and basil.

Makes about 3 cups, or 6 ½-cup servings of 49 calories each.

Covered, can be refrigerated up to 4 days; frozen, up to 3 months.

Grapefruit Vinaigrette

1 small grapefruit (or 1 large navel orange), peeled, pith removed with serrated knife; in sections with skin and seeds removed
1 small shallot

2 tsp extra virgin olive oil*
2 tsp raspberry or white wine vinegar
1 Tbsp fresh chives, chopped
       black pepper, freshly ground, to taste

In blender or food processor combine all ingredients except chives and pepper; process until smooth. Stir in chives; season with pepper.

Makes ½ cup, or 4 2-Tbsp servings of 49 calories each.

Can be refrigerated, covered, up to 3 days.

*See note page 101.

Pesto Sauce with Lemon

4 garlic cloves
3 cups fresh basil leaves, packed
2 cups spinach leaves, trimmed, packed

3 Tbsp Parmesan cheese, freshly grated
2 Tbsp pine nuts
¼ tsp black pepper, freshly ground
¼ cup extra virgin olive oil*
2 Tbsp fresh lemon juice

In food processor mince garlic. Add basil, spinach, cheese, nuts and pepper; purée. With machine running, slowly pour in oil and juice; process until smooth.

Makes about 1 cup, or 8 2-Tbsp servings of 92 calories each.

Covered, can be refrigerated up to 2 weeks; or frozen up to 3 months — pour 1 tsp olive oil over before freezing.

*See note page 101.

33

Piquant Ranch Salsa

Lends spice to grilled seafood or vegetables.

1 cup   tomatoes, diced
¼ cup   green onion, minced
2 Tbsp   red onion, chopped

1 Tbsp   fresh lemon or lime juice
1 Tbsp   fresh cilantro, chopped
1   medium jalapeño chile,* minced (or ½ tsp dried chili flakes)
1   large garlic clove, minced
          black pepper, freshly ground, to taste

In medium bowl combine all ingredients. Season and refrigerate to allow flavors to meld. Let sit 1 hour at room temperature before serving. Makes about 1½ cups, or 6 ¼-cup servings of 22 calories each.
*See note page 101.

Tomatillo Salsa with Cilantro

1½ lbs   fresh tomatillos,* husked and rinsed
1 cup   onions, chopped
1 cup   White Vegetable Stock (page 18)

2 Tbsp   fresh garlic, minced
½   medium jalapeño chile,** chopped
¼ cup   fresh parsley leaves, lightly packed
1 Tbsp   fresh lemon or lime juice
1 Tbsp   cilantro, minced

Lightly toast all vegetables over flame or in a very hot, dry sauté pan until lightly charred. In medium pan combine tomatillos, onions, Stock, garlic and chile. Bring to boil; simmer, covered, over medium-low heat 15 minutes. In blender or food processor purée sauce and other ingredients until smooth.

Makes about 2½ cups, or 10 ¼-cup servings of 69 calories each.

Covered, can be refrigerated up to 5 days; or frozen up to 3 months.

*See note page 102.
**See note page 101.

Yellow Pepper Sauce

2 yellow bell peppers, quartered	
1¼ cups White Vegetable Stock (page 18)	1 large shallot, minced
	4 thyme sprigs

In saucepan combine all ingredients and simmer 15 minutes, or until peppers are tender. Remove thyme.

Purée in blender until smooth. Reheat before serving.

Serve with Fresh Squash Blossoms Filled with Fromage Blanc (page 77), or favorite fish dish.

Makes 4 servings—calories negligible.

Yogurt-Cucumber Dressing

	1 medium green onion, cut in 1" pcs
	¼ cup low-fat plain yogurt or cottage cheese
1 medium cucumber (about ½ lb), peeled; halved lengthwise, seeded, cut in 1" pcs	2 Tbsp fresh lemon juice
	1 Tbsp white wine vinegar
	1 garlic clove, halved
¼ cup fresh parsley leaves, packed	black pepper, freshly ground, to taste

In food processor or blender combine all ingredients (except pepper) until smooth. Season.

Makes 1 cup, or 8 2-Tbsp servings of 12 calories each.

Can be refrigerated, covered, up to 3 days.

Roasted chile-cheese custard.

Luncheon Entrées & Pastas

Baked Pasta Casserole

3 qts	water	⅓ cup	Parmesan or Romano cheese, freshly grated
8 oz	dry whole-wheat, tomato or spinach (or mixed) medium pasta shells, or fusilli noodles	4	sun-dried tomatoes,* rinsed of oil, patted dry and chopped
1	small onion, chopped	2 Tbsp	fresh oregano, chopped (or 1½ tsp dried leaves)
½ lb	fresh mushrooms, domestic or wild, cut in ½" slices	3 Tbsp	fresh basil, chopped (or 1½ tsp dried leaves)
3	garlic cloves, minced	1½ cups	Fresh Tomato-Basil Sauce (page 32)
½ lb	zucchini (1 medium), cut into ½" dice		black pepper, freshly ground, to taste
½ cup	part-skim mozzarella cheese (1¼ oz), freshly grated	½ cup	part-skim mozzarella cheese (1¼ oz), freshly grated

In large pot bring water to boil. Add pasta; boil 6-8 minutes or until just tender. Drain pasta; place in large bowl. Preheat oven to 350.°

Heat medium pan over medium-high heat; lightly brush with vegetable oil. Add onion, mushrooms and garlic; cook, stirring frequently, until soft, about 4-5 minutes. Transfer vegetables to pasta bowl. Lightly brush pan with oil; add zucchini. Sauté over medium-high heat until zucchini browns and softens, about 3 minutes. Add zucchini to pasta. Stir in ½ cup mozzarella cheese, Parmesan cheese, tomatoes, herbs and 1 cup Tomato Sauce. Season with pepper.

Transfer pasta to 2½- to 3-qt casserole dish. Spread remaining Tomato Sauce over pasta; sprinkle remaining mozzarella over sauce. Bake covered casserole 10 minutes. Remove cover; bake 5 minutes more. Let sit 5 minutes; serve.

Makes about 6 1⅓-cup servings of 255 calories each.

*See note page 102.

Cobb Salad

		½ lb	broccoli, peeled, trimmed, cut in 1″ florets; steamed until tender
4 cups	assorted lettuce leaves, torn		
2 cups	tofu (about ½ lb), diced, drained	1 cup	tomato (about 2 medium), diced
1⅓ cups	brown rice, cooked	1 cup	cucumber (1 small), peeled, diced
2	large eggs, hardboiled, diced	1 cup	carrots (1 medium), peeled, diced
½ cup	low-sodium Cheddar cheese; freshly grated (1¼ oz)	1 cup	zucchini (1 medium), diced

Place lettuce on 4 plates. Onto center of each spoon ½ cup tofu, ⅓ cup rice, 2-3 Tbsp egg and 2 Tbsp cheese. Divide onto plates broccoli, tomato, cucumber, carrots and zucchini. Serve chilled, with Creamy Ranch (page 31) or Yogurt-Cucumber (page 35) Dressing.

Makes 4 servings of 205 calories each.

Fettucini Alfredo

½ cup	nonfat plain yogurt		
½ cup	nonfat cottage cheese	12 oz	dried fettucini, cooked al dente
1 tsp	fresh garlic, diced		
½ tsp	lemon zest,* minced	2 Tbsp	fresh parsley, chopped
⅛ tsp	black pepper, freshly ground	⅛ cup	low-fat Parmesan cheese, freshly grated

In blender combine yogurt, cottage cheese, garlic, lemon zest and black pepper. Blend on high till creamy. Set aside.

In mixing bowl place hot pasta, drained. Toss with parsley and Parmesan cheese. Combine pasta and cream mixture. Toss and serve.

Makes 4 servings of 239 calories each.

*See note page 102.

Lentil and Mushroom Enchiladas

1 tsp	canola or olive oil*
1	bay leaf
⅓ cup	onion, chopped
2	garlic cloves, minced
¼ tsp	dried chili flakes
1⅓ cups	White Vegetable Stock (page 18) or water
½ cup	lentils, sorted
1 lb	fresh mushrooms, cut into ½" slices
1 cup	onion, chopped

1	bay leaf
2	garlic cloves, minced
2 Tbsp	fresh oregano, chopped
2 Tbsp	fresh basil, chopped
¼ cup	fresh cilantro, chopped
	black pepper, freshly ground, to taste
6	corn or whole-wheat tortillas (about 7-8" diameter)
2-3 cups	Ancho Chile Sauce (page 30)
1 cup	low-sodium cheddar cheese (2½ oz) or Monterey Jack, freshly grated

Sauté onion, garlic, chili flakes and bay leaf in large pot over medium heat until onion is golden. Add Stock and bring to boil; stir in lentils. Cook, covered, over low heat 20-25 minutes or until lentils are just tender. Do not overcook. Remove bay leaf. Drain any liquid from lentils. Preheat oven to 350.°

In large pan combine mushrooms, onion, bay leaf and garlic. Cook, covered, until onions are soft, about 3 minutes. Remove cover; cook vegetables until liquid from mushrooms evaporates, about 5 minutes. Remove bay leaf. Transfer mix to large bowl; stir in oregano, basil, cilantro and lentils. Season with pepper.

On large baking sheet arrange tortillas in 1 layer; cover with damp kitchen towel and bake until tortillas are warm not crisp, about 4-5 minutes. Spread about 2 Tbsp Ancho Chile Sauce on each tortilla. Spoon about ½ cup filling in its center; wrap up like a crêpe.

Lightly brush baking sheet with vegetable oil. Set enchiladas on sheet; spoon 1 cup Ancho Chile Sauce over them, then sprinkle with cheese. Bake 15 minutes or until heated through and cheese melts. Serve hot with additional Ancho Chile Sauce.

Makes 6 servings of 145 calories each.

*Non-stick vegetable spray may be used to lightly coat the pot.

Pasta Primavera with Lemony Pesto

3 qts	water
8 oz	dry whole-wheat, spinach or tomato (or mixed) medium pasta shells or fusilli pasta
1	large zucchini, cut lengthwise in thin 2" strips
1	large yellow squash, cut lengthwise in thin 2" strips

¾ cup	Pesto Sauce with Lemon (page 33)
1	large red or green bell pepper, cut in thin strips
2	medium tomatoes, coarsely chopped
2	green onions, coarsely chopped
2 Tbsp	fresh parsley, chopped
¼ cup	Parmesan cheese, freshly grated
	black pepper, freshly ground, to taste

In large pot bring water to boil. Add pasta; boil 6 minutes or until almost tender. Add squashes; boil 1 minute. Drain pasta and vegetables well; transfer to large bowl and toss with ½ cup Pesto. Add all remaining ingredients except black pepper; toss until well combined. Season with pepper. Serve chilled or at room temperature.

Makes about 6 1¼-cup servings of 200 calories each.

Can be refrigerated, covered, up to 3 days.

Roasted Chile-Cheese Custard

		4	large eggs
		⅔ cup	non-fat yogurt
1 14-oz can	roasted whole green chiles (or 2 7-oz cans)*	½ tsp	ground cumin
		⅛ tsp	black pepper, freshly ground
1 cup	tomato, diced	¼ tsp	garlic powder
½ cup	green onions, chopped	⅔ cup	low-sodium Cheddar cheese (1½ oz), freshly grated
large pinch	cayenne pepper		

Preheat oven to 375.° Lightly brush with vegetable oil 9″ heat-proof glass pie dish. Chop 2 chiles; combine with tomatoes, green onions and cayenne pepper. In large bowl whisk eggs, yogurt, cumin, black pepper and garlic powder. Slit remaining chiles lengthwise; open flat; arrange 4 over base and sides of pie dish. Spoon ½ tomato mixture over chiles. Sprinkle with ½ of cheese and pour over ⅔ cup egg mix. For final layer repeat: remaining chiles, tomato mix, cheese, and egg mix. Bake 25-30 minutes or until lightly brown, puffed and set at center. Let sit 10 minutes; serve.

Makes 4 servings of 210 calories each.

*See note page 101.

Spinach-Cheese Quesadillas

4	corn tortillas (7-8″ diameter)
1 large bunch	fresh spinach, rinsed, stems removed, patted dry (or 4 oz frozen leaf spinach, thawed and pressed dry), chopped
¼ cup	green onion, minced
¼ cup	tomatoes, chopped
1	garlic clove, minced
1 Tbsp	fresh lemon juice
½ tsp	ground cumin
½ cup	Monterey Jack cheese (1¼ oz) or mild low-sodium Cheddar, freshly grated
2 Tbsp	low-fat ricotta cheese
2 Tbsp	tofu (firm), drained and crumbled
2 Tbsp	fresh cilantro, minced
	black pepper, freshly ground, to taste

In medium skillet combine spinach, onion, tomatoes, garlic, lemon juice and cumin. Cook over low heat until liquid is absorbed, about 5 minutes. Transfer to medium bowl; add ¼ cup Monterey Jack, plus ricotta cheese, tofu and cilantro. Season with pepper.

Divide and spoon filling on 2 tortillas. Sprinkle remaining ¼ cup Monterey Jack over filling; place a tortilla over cheese. Set non-stick pan (8-10″ diameter) over low heat; heat both sides of each quesadilla until lightly brown and cheese melts. Cut each quesadilla into 4 wedges. Serve warm.

Makes 4 2-wedge servings of 125 calories each.

Stuffed Tomato with Tuna Salad

13 oz water-packed albacore (2 6½-oz cans), drained
½ cup green onion, chopped
3 Tbsp fresh lemon juice
¼ cup low-fat cottage cheese (or low-fat plain yogurt)
1½ Tbsp Dijon-type mustard*
2 Tbsp fresh dill, parsley or cilantro, chopped

black pepper, freshly ground, to taste
2 large tomatoes, cored and halved crosswise
2 cups medium cauliflower florets
2 cups medium broccoli florets
½ lb asparagus spears, trimmed
4 cups assorted lettuce leaves, torn, rinsed and spun dry
2 lemons, halved (garnish)

In medium bowl mix first 6 ingredients well. Season. Set aside.

Scoop tomato meat from halves, leaving ½″ border. Dice tomato meat; reserve. Steam next 3 vegetables until just tender; chill. Arrange lettuce on 4 plates. In each plate center tomato half; spoon on ¾ cup tuna. Top with reserved diced tomato. Divide cooked vegetables onto plates. Chill. Garnish and serve.

Makes 4 servings of 227 calories each.

*See note page 101.

Tempeh Reuben Sandwich

1 tempeh patty
4 tsp Dijon-type mustard*
4 slices whole-wheat/rye bread

1 oz low-fat low-sodium Swiss cheese (2 slices)
1 large sweet onion, sliced
1 cup low-sodium sauerkraut, drained
4 slices tomato
nonstick vegetable spray

Halve tempeh patty crosswise. Grill until lightly charred. Spread mustard over bread. Layer tempeh, cheese, onion, sauerkraut and tomato over 2 bread slices. Cover with remaining bread.

Heat large nonstick pan; spray lightly. Brown both sides of sandwich and melt cheese.

Halve each sandwich. Serve hot with low-sodium pickles or cucumbers.

Makes 4 servings of 149 calories each.

*See note page 101.

Toasted Cheese and Tomato Sandwich

		1	small tomato, cut in 1/4" slices
		1/4 cup	green onion, chopped
		1/2 cup	Monterey Jack cheese (1 1/4 oz) or part-skim mozzarella, freshly grated
4 slices	Tecate Ranch Whole-Wheat Bread (page 88)		

Lightly toast bread. Set on medium baking sheet. On each slice layer 1 tomato slice, 1 Tbsp onion and 2 Tbsp cheese.

Preheat oven to 350°–or broil. Heat until cheese melts but does not brown and sandwich heats through.

Makes 4 servings of 148 calories each.

Whole-Wheat Pizza Dough

		1 tsp	garlic
		2 tsp	wild sage honey
3/4 cup plus 2 Tbsp	warm water 110-115°	1 packet	active dry yeast (1/4 oz)
2 tsp	olive oil*	1 cup	whole-wheat flour**
1 tsp	oregano	1 cup	all-purpose unbleached flour**
1 tsp	dried basil	1/4 tsp	sea salt

In small bowl combine water, oil, herbs, garlic and honey. Stir in yeast to dissolve. Let stand until frothy, about 5 minutes. In large bowl combine flours and salt. Pour yeast mix over flour; stir until combined. Transfer dough to floured surface. Knead dough until smooth and soft; shape into ball. Set in large bowl lightly brushed with vegetable oil; turn dough once. Cover bowl of dough. Allow to rise in warm place about 45 minutes, until double in volume. Divide into 6 pcs. Knead each ball until smooth. Roll out dough balls as needed for pizza.

Makes 6 3 1/2-oz pizzas of 159 calories each.

*See note page 101.

**See note page 102.

Vegetable Pizza

1 recipe	Whole-Wheat Pizza Dough (page 45)
1½ cups	Fresh Tomato-Basil Sauce (page 32)
¼ cup	fresh basil, chopped (or 3 Tbsp dried leaves)
3 Tbsp	fresh oregano, chopped (or 1½ tsp dried leaves)
6 tsp	Parmesan cheese, freshly grated
3	small zucchini, cut in ¼″ slices
2	medium green or red bell peppers, cut in thin strips
8 oz	fresh mushrooms, thinly sliced
½	small red onion, thinly sliced
¾ cup	part-skim mozzarella cheese (2 oz), freshly grated

Preheat oven to 425°. Lightly brush 2 large baking sheets with vegetable oil. Roll each ball of dough into 7″ circle, flouring if dough sticks to working surface. Set rolled dough on baking sheets. Fold over edges of dough by ½″ to make rim; crimp. Set dough aside to rise for 15 minutes.

Spoon ¼ cup Tomato-Basil Sauce over each pizza; sprinkle with basil, oregano and 1 tsp Parmesan. Evenly divide vegetables over pizzas; top with 2 Tbsp mozzarella. Bake 20 minutes or until crusts are golden.

Makes 6 pizzas of 223 calories each.

Variation: Grilled Eggplant and Goat-Cheese Pizza with Thyme

1 recipe	Whole-Wheat Pizza Dough (page 45)
1	eggplant (about 1 lb), cut crosswise in ½″ slices
2 bunches	spinach, trimmed and rinsed; cooked and pressed dry
1½ cups	Fresh Tomato-Basil Sauce (page 32)
2 tsp	fresh thyme leaves
⅓ cup	mild goat cheese (about 2 oz), crumbled

Follow Vegetable Pizza directions (page 46). Lightly brush both sides of eggplant with vegetable oil; broil or grill, turning until tender.

Preheat oven to 425°. Layer rolled doughs with spinach, eggplant, Tomato-Basil Sauce, thyme and cheese. Bake 20 minutes.

Makes 6 pizzas of 233 calories each.

Variation: Mushroom and Parmesan-Cheese Pizza with Fennel Seed

1 recipe	Whole-Wheat Pizza Dough (page 45)
1 lb	fresh mushrooms, cut in ½" slices
2	garlic cloves, minced
1 recipe	Fresh Tomato-Basil Sauce (page 32)
1 tsp	fennel seed
2 tsp	fresh thyme leaves
6 tsp	Parmesan cheese, freshly grated

Follow Vegetable Pizza directions (page 46).

Over medium-high heat sauté mushrooms with garlic until liquid is absorbed.

Preheat oven to 425.° Spread rolled doughs with 1½ cups Tomato-Basil Sauce (save remaining sauce for other use or freeze). Sprinkle with fennel and thyme, spoon over mushrooms, top with cheese. Bake 20 minutes.

Makes 6 pizzas of 214 calories each.

Variation: Tomato and Pesto Pizza

1 recipe	Whole-Wheat Pizza Dough (page 46)
1 recipe	Pesto Sauce with Lemon (page 33)
½	small red onion, thinly sliced
4	medium tomatoes (or a variety of red and yellow tomatoes), cut in ½" slices
1 cup	part-skim mozzarella cheese (about 3 oz), freshly grated

Follow Vegetable Pizza directions (page 46). Spread rolled doughs with 6 Tbsp Pesto Sauce. Save remaining Pesto Sauce for other use or freeze.

Preheat oven to 425.° Layer doughs with onion, tomatoes and cheese. Bake 20 minutes.

Makes 6 pizzas of 276 calories each.

Variation: Zucchini and Sun-Dried Tomato Pizza with Mozzarella Cheese

1 recipe   Whole-Wheat Pizza
           Dough (page 45)

1 recipe   Fresh Tomato-Basil
           Sauce (page 32)
½ cup   fresh basil, chopped
4   medium zucchini (2 lbs),
           sliced diagonally in pcs
           3-4″ long, ¼″ thick
6   sun-dried tomatoes,*
           rinsed of oil, sliced in
           thin strips
3 oz   part-skim mozzarella
           cheese (about 1 cup),
           freshly grated

Follow Vegetable Pizza directions (page 46).

Broil or grill zucchini until brown on both sides.

Preheat oven to 425.° Spread rolled doughs with 1½ cups Tomato-Basil Sauce (save remaining sauce for other use). Sprinkle with basil; layer with zucchini, tomatoes and cheese. Bake 20 minutes.

Makes 6 pizzas of 237 calories each.

*See note page 102.

Dining Room—
Rancho La Puerta
1950

Layered tamale pie with corn, tomatoes and cheese.

Dinner Entrées & Seafood

Baked Eggplant Gratin with Ricotta Soufflé

2 lbs	eggplant, trimmed
¼ cup	White Vegetable Stock (page 18)
1 Tbsp	olive oil*
2 Tbsp	fresh parsley, chopped
2 Tbsp	fresh thyme or basil, chopped; or 1 tsp dried
4	garlic cloves, crushed

Ricotta Cheese Custard:

2 cups	low-fat ricotta cheese
2	eggs
2	egg whites
½ cup	Parmesan cheese, freshly grated
⅔ cup	low-fat milk
hvy pinch	ground nutmeg
hvy pinch	black pepper, freshly ground
hvy pinch	cayenne pepper
1 tsp	dried basil, crumbled
2½-3 cups	Fresh Tomato-Basil Sauce (page 32)
1	small bunch fresh basil, torn into pcs

Preheat broiler. Slice eggplant into ½"-crosswise pieces; lightly mark both sides with X, using knife.

In small bowl combine Stock, oil, parsley, thyme and garlic. Brush each eggplant slice with herb mixture. Place slices on baking sheet; broil or grill until well browned.

Preheat oven to 400°. In large bowl combine ricotta cheese, egg and egg whites. Whisk in Parmesan cheese and milk. Season to taste, with nutmeg, black pepper, cayenne and dried basil. Set aside.

In each of 8 small gratin dishes spoon ¼ cup Tomato-Basil Sauce, 3-4 eggplant slices, ⅛ of torn basil and ⅛ of ricotta-cheese mixture.

Bake 10 minutes; reduce heat to 375° and bake 10-15 minutes, until puffy and very brown on top.

Makes 8 servings of 170 calories each.

*See note page 101.

Baked Sea Bass in Romaine with California Salsa

1 Tbsp green onion, diced
2 tsp   chives, diced
2 tsp   cilantro, chopped
1 tsp   fresh lime juice
½ tsp   dried chili flakes
dash   Tabasco sauce, to taste

California Salsa:

1 cup   tomatoes, peeled, seeded and diced
¼ cup   bell peppers, finely diced
2 Tbsp white onion, diced
2 Tbsp radish sprouts

4   sea bass fillets (about 5 oz ea)
4   large romaine lettuce leaves
1   lime, sliced (garnish)

In medium-size bowl combine all salsa ingredients; mix well. Let stand 1 hour at room temperature.

Preheat oven to 375°.

Dip each lettuce leaf in boiling water 1½ minutes. Drain; pat dry with paper towel. Place 1 fillet on each lettuce leaf. Spoon 2 Tbsp Salsa over each. Fold lettuce over fillet to cover completely.

Place fillets in lightly oiled baking pan. Bake, covered, 20 minutes. Then insert skewer through lettuce and fish. If skewer is hot after removal, fish is done.

Spoon remaining Salsa over fillets. Garnish and serve.

Makes 4 servings of 165 calories each.

Black-Bean Flauta with Two Sauces

½ cup	dried black beans,* sorted and rinsed
4 cups	White Vegetable Stock (page 18)
½ cup	onion, chopped
2 Tbsp	garlic, minced
1	medium jalapeño chile, minced**
1½ tsp	ground cumin
1	bay leaf
1¼ tsp	dried oregano leaves
¼ tsp	sea salt
¼ tsp	black pepper, freshly ground
4	corn or whole-wheat tortillas (6-7″ diameter)
½ cup	green onion, chopped
¼ cup	tomatoes, finely diced
½ cup	part-skim mozzarella cheese (1¼ oz), freshly grated
½	small tomato, cut into thin strips (garnish)
1	green onion, cut into thin strips (garnish)
½ cup	Ancho Chile Sauce (page 30)

In small bowl cover beans with water by 4″; refrigerate overnight; drain. In medium pot combine Stock, onion, garlic, chile, 1 tsp cumin, bay leaf, 1 tsp oregano, salt and pepper. Bring to boil; stir in beans; cook, covered, over low heat until beans are tender, about 45 minutes. Remove bay leaf. Drain beans, reserving liquid.

Preheat oven to 400°. On large baking sheet arrange tortillas in 1 layer. Bake, covered with moist kitchen towel, until warm but not crisp, about 4-5 minutes.

In center of each tortilla spoon 2 Tbsp beans, top with 2 Tbsp green onion, 1 Tbsp tomato and 2 Tbsp cheese. Roll up tortillas, place seam-side down in medium baking dish. Bake, uncovered, 10-15 minutes or until flautas are crispy brown.

In blender or food processor purée remaining beans with 4-6 Tbsp reserved bean liquid. Season, if desired, with remaining ½ tsp cumin and ¼ tsp oregano.

Partially cover 1 side of each flauta with 2 Tbsp puréed sauce; alongside, spoon 2 Tbsp Ancho Chile Sauce. Garnish. Serve hot.

Makes 4 servings of 187 calories each.

*For dried beans, substitute 1½ cups canned black beans (rinsed and drained) in medium pot, combined with 1 cup White Vegetable Stock, 1 Tbsp garlic, 1 tsp cumin, ½ tsp oregano and 1 bay leaf. Simmer, covered, 15 minutes. Remove bay leaf. Drain beans, reserving cooking liquid. Then proceed as directed.

**See note page 101.

Charbroiled Swordfish with Red Bell Pepper-Saffron Sauce

¼ cup	carrots, diced
¼ cup	celery, diced
¼ tsp	fresh garlic, minced
½ tsp	saffron threads
¼ tsp	ground nutmeg
⅛ tsp	cayenne pepper
¼ tsp	ground cloves

¼ cup	dry white wine
2 cups	red bell pepper, diced
¼ cup	green bell pepper, diced
¼ cup	onion, diced
3 cups	White Vegetable Stock (page 18)
½ cup	low-fat cottage cheese
4	swordfish fillets (ea 4 oz)
1	lime, sliced (garnish)

In 2-qt saucepan combine wine, red and green peppers, onion, carrots, celery and garlic. Cook, covered, over low heat 5-10 minutes until vegetables are softened. Stir in saffron threads and other seasonings. Add Stock and simmer, covered, 45 minutes over low heat.

In blender combine cottage cheese and ¼ of vegetable mixture. Blend until smooth. Add remaining vegetable mixture and blend until very smooth. Set aside; keep warm.

Place swordfish on grill. Cook 1 minute. Lift and turn fillets 90°, for crisscross pattern. Grill 1 minute more. Turn fillets over, repeating process.

Place swordfish on 4 individual serving plates; top each with 2 Tbsp sauce. Garnish and serve.

Makes 4 servings of 252 calories each.

Chiles Rellenos

4 California chiles*
(4 oz ea)
4 oz low-fat Monterey Jack
cheese, cut in 4 sticks
4 oz low-fat Monterey Jack
cheese, freshly grated
4 Tbsp whole-wheat flour**
4 egg whites, beaten until
fluffy
1 egg yolk
non-stick vegetable spray
8 oz Ancho Chile Sauce
(page 30) or Tomatillo
Salsa (page 34)

Roast chiles in 400° oven until dark in color. Cool to room temperature and peel skin. Rinse each chile in cold water.

Cut pocket to remove seeds. Fill each chile with cheese stick. Sprinkle over 1 Tbsp flour.

Whip egg whites and yolk separately, then fold together. They should be very thick. Dip each chile into egg mixture.

In sprayed non-stick pan sauté chiles slowly until batter is golden brown.

Finish cooking in 350° oven, until soft. Cover each chile with 2 oz sauce. Sprinkle with grated cheese. Return to oven to melt cheese. Serve immediately.

Makes 4 servings of 202 calories each.

*See note page 101.

**See note page 102.

Layered Tamale Pie with Corn, Tomatoes and Cheese

¾ cup	dried red or kidney beans** (or 2 cups–1 20-oz can–kidney beans, undrained)
1	large onion, chopped
4	garlic cloves, minced
1	medium jalapeño* or serrano chile, minced
2	green bell peppers, diced
2	large carrots, peeled, diced in ½" pcs
1½ Tbsp	dried oregano leaves
1 Tbsp	ground cumin
1 cup	corn kernels, fresh or frozen
6	medium tomatoes, chopped (or 1 28-oz can crushed tomatoes)
	black pepper, freshly ground, to taste
1 cup	yellow cornmeal
2½ cups	water
1 cup	low-fat milk
	black pepper, freshly ground, to taste
2 cups	low-sodium Cheddar like Tillamook (5 oz) or Monterey Jack cheese, freshly grated
6 Tbsp	cilantro, chopped (garnish)

Drain cooked beans; reserve ½ cup liquid. In large pan combine onion, garlic, chile, bell peppers, carrots, oregano, cumin and reserved bean liquid. Cook, covered, over medium heat until vegetables are soft and liquid absorbed, about 10-15 minutes. Add cooked beans, corn and tomatoes; cook, uncovered, stirring occasionally, until mix thickens, about 15 minutes. Season bean mix with black pepper; stir in 4 Tbsp cilantro. Preheat oven to 350.°

In medium saucepan combine cornmeal, water and milk; bring to boil over low heat; cook, stirring constantly, until thickened, about 4-5 minutes. Season with black pepper. Cover and stir before layering pie.

In 2-qt baking dish pour ½ vegetable-bean mix; then spread ½ cornmeal mix; sprinkle with half of cheese. Repeat; in final layer use remaining vegetable-bean mix, cornmeal mix and cheese. Bake 25 minutes or until bubbly hot. Garnish and serve.

Makes 8 servings of 233 calories each.

*See note page 101.

**To cook dried beans: Rinse and sort. In medium bowl cover beans with water by 4"; refrigerate overnight; drain. In medium pot combine beans with 5½ cups White Vegetable Stock (page 18) or water. Cook, covered, over medium-low heat until beans are tender, about 1½ hours.

Marinated Tofu "Steaks" with Pineapple Salsa

Marinade:

⅔ cup   White Vegetable Stock (page 18)

¼ cup   fresh lemon juice or white wine

1 Tbsp   dried chili flakes or 4 jalapeño chiles, cut in ½" slices*

1   bunch cilantro, finely chopped

¼ cup   fresh ginger, minced

black pepper, freshly ground, to taste

10   garlic cloves, smashed, peel removed

1¼ lbs   firm tofu, drained, cut into 4 1"-lengthwise "steaks"

Pineapple or Mango Salsa:

1   small pineapple or 1 medium mango (about ¾ lb), ripe

1 Tbsp   cilantro, chopped

½   jalapeño chile, seeds and ribs removed, minced*

4   large cilantro sprigs (garnish)

4   thin avocado slices (garnish)

Preheat grill or broiler.

In medium baking dish combine marinade ingredients. Pat tofu dry with paper toweling. Add tofu to marinade, 2-3 hours at room temperature or refrigerate overnight. Peel pineapple; chop very fine. Place in medium bowl with remaining salsa ingredients. Set aside 1 hour at room temperature; transfer to serving bowl.

Lightly oil barbecue grills or broiler pan. Lightly char tofu steaks (3-4 minutes each side), basting constantly. Garnish. Serve tofu steaks with a side of salsa.

Makes 4 servings of 154 calories each.

*See note page 101.

Mock Swordfish with Ancho Chile Sauce and Spinach

4	4-oz firm tofu cakes, about 1″ thick; drained
2 bunches	spinach, stems removed; cooked, pressed dry, coarsely chopped
1 cup	Ancho Chile Sauce (page 30)
½ cup	low-sodium Gouda or part-skim mozzarella cheese (1½ oz), freshly grated
1½ cups	White Vegetable Stock (page 18)
3 Tbsp	fresh lemon juice
6	medium jalapeño chiles,* chopped (or 2 tsp dried chili flakes)
2 Tbsp	cold-pressed sesame oil
1 small bunch	cilantro, rinsed, chopped
8	garlic cloves, chopped
¼ cup	fresh ginger, grated

In medium-shallow dish combine last 7 ingredients. Cover tofu in this marinade 4 hours at room temperature or overnight in refrigerator. Drain tofu. Reserve marinade.

Preheat broiler or barbecue grill. Broil tofu, brushing with reserved marinade, about 4 minutes each side or until lightly charred.

Preheat oven to 400°.

In each of 4 small heat-proof gratin or similar serving dishes place about ¼ cup spinach. Top with 1 tofu cake, then with ¼ cup Ancho Chile Sauce. Sprinkle with 2 Tbsp cheese. Bake until cheese is melted but not brown and tofu heated through. Serve hot in gratin dishes.

Makes 4 servings of 165 calories each.

*See note page 101.

Poached Sole with Dill Sauce

Dill Sauce:

7 oz	soft tofu, drained on paper towels
½ cup	low-fat buttermilk
½ cup	fresh dill sprigs
⅛ tsp	ground nutmeg
⅛ tsp	Worcestershire sauce

1 tsp	shallots, diced
2 Tbsp	fresh lemon juice
¼ tsp	salt
1 Tbsp	olive oil*
¼ cup	celery, chopped
¼ cup	carrots, chopped
¼ cup	onion, sliced
4	sole fillets (each 4 oz)
	water
	fresh dill sprigs (garnish)

Process all sauce ingredients in blender until smooth. Scrape down sides and process until very smooth.

In large sauté pan combine celery, carrots and onion. Place sole fillets on top vegetables. Add water to cover. Simmer, covered, 5-8 minutes, or until sole flakes.

With slotted spoon transfer fillets to heated serving plates. Spoon 2 Tbsp Dill Sauce over each fillet. Garnish and serve.

Serve with Four-Grain Pilaf (page 69)

Makes 4 servings of 251 calories each, without Pilaf.

*See note page 101.

Scampi Provençal

1 Tbsp	olive oil*
16	large raw shrimp, shelled and deveined
3	tomatoes, diced
¼ cup	green onions, diced
1 tsp	fresh garlic, minced
2 Tbsp	fresh parsley, chopped
2 Tbsp	fresh lemon juice
¼ cup	dry white wine

In medium skillet heat oil. Sauté shrimp until opaque, about 1 minute. Add tomatoes, onion, garlic and parsley. Stir and heat about 3 minutes, until shrimp are pink. Add lemon juice and wine; bring to boil. Remove from heat.

Serve with ½ cup prepared wild rice.

Makes 4 servings of 132 calories each. (With rice, 222 calories each.)

*See note page 101.

Snapper Veracruz

Zesty and colorful: pair this entrée with Ancho Chile (page 30) and Tomatillo Salsa (page 34)

	black pepper, freshly ground, to taste
3 Tbsp	fresh lemon or lime juice
4	5-oz red snapper, halibut or swordfish fillets, 1" thick
¼ cup	fresh cilantro, chopped
¼ cup	dry white wine
8	garlic cloves, crushed, peels removed
1	medium jalapeño chile,* coarsely chopped
2	shallots, chopped

Rub fish with garlic, season with black pepper. In small bowl combine garlic with remaining ingredients. In medium-shallow dish set fish, pour marinade over. Let stand, covered, 1 hour at room temperature; or refrigerate overnight.

Preheat broiler or barbecue grill. Remove fish from marinade, scraping off any remaining chile or garlic. Broil or grill fish, basting with marinade, 4-5 minutes each side or until fish is lightly charred and opaque. Do not overcook.

Makes 4 servings of 184 calories each.

*See note page 101.

61

Stuffed Baked Potato with Broccoli

2	large baking potatoes (about 1 lb)	2 Tbsp	Parmesan cheese, freshly grated
¼ cup	low-fat cottage cheese	1 Tbsp	fresh chives, minced
2 Tbsp	low-fat plain yogurt	2 tsp	Dijon-type mustard*
2 Tbsp	low-fat milk	⅛ tsp	white pepper, or to taste
		¼ cup	part-skim mozzarella cheese, freshly grated
		1½ cups	medium broccoli florets, steamed until just tender (garnish)

Preheat oven to 375°. In medium baking dish set potatoes; cover with foil; bake 1 hour or until tender. Halve potatoes lengthwise and scoop out, leaving ½" border. In bowl of food processor mix scooped potato with remaining ingredients, except mozzarella and broccoli, about 5-10 seconds or until just smooth; or mash filling in mixing bowl until smooth.

Refill potato skins. Divide mozzarella and broccoli florets over each potato. In medium covered baking dish bake potatoes 10 minutes or until cheese melts and potatoes are hot.

Makes 4 servings of 165 calories each.

*See note page 101.

Stuffed Bell Peppers with Bulgur Wheat and Tofu

4 medium green or red bell peppers

1½ cups	White Vegetable Stock (page 18)
1½ tsp	fresh marjoram
2 tsp	fresh thyme
2 tsp	fresh rosemary
¼ tsp	salt
1 cup	bulgur wheat
4 oz	firm tofu, drained and diced
½ cup	tomato, diced

Preheat oven to 350°.

Cut off pepper tops and reserve; remove pepper seeds and white membranes. Blanch peppers 2 minutes and drain, cut side down, on paper toweling. Pat insides dry. Set peppers aside.

In medium saucepot combine Stock, marjoram, thyme, rosemary and salt. Bring to boil, and stir in bulgur wheat; reduce heat and simmer, covered, 10 minutes. Remove from heat. Stir in tofu and tomato. Stuff peppers with bulgur mixture; replace tops. In medium heat-proof dish bake peppers, covered, 20-25 minutes or until tender.

Makes 4 servings of 207 calories each.

Whole-Wheat Lasagne with Spinach and Mushrooms

2 bunches	spinach (2 lbs) trimmed, rinsed (or 32 oz frozen leaf spinach, thawed), pressed to remove water, chopped
3 qts	water
6 oz	dried whole-wheat or spinach lasagne noodles
1 Tbsp	pure olive oil*
1	small onion, thinly sliced
6 oz	fresh mushrooms, sliced
1	bell pepper, julienned
1	carrot, shredded
2	garlic cloves, minced
1 Tbsp	fresh basil, chopped (or 1 tsp dried leaves)
1 Tbsp	fresh oregano, chopped (or ½ tsp dried leaves)
	black pepper, freshly ground, to taste
1½ cups	low-fat ricotta cheese
3 Tbsp	Parmesan cheese, freshly grated
1	large egg
1	large egg white
2 Tbsp	fresh parsley, chopped
pinch	ground nutmeg
	black pepper, freshly ground, to taste
2½ cups	Fresh Tomato-Basil Sauce (page 32)
¾ cup	part-skim mozzarella cheese (2 oz), freshly grated

In large pan cook spinach, with water still clinging to leaves, till wilted. Press to remove water. Chop. Set aside. In large pot bring water to boil. Add noodles, cook 8-10 minutes or until tender. Drain, rinse. Preheat oven to 400.°

In medium pan heat oil; add onions, mushrooms, bell pepper and carrot; sauté over low heat until onions are soft and mixture is almost dry, about 10 minutes. Add garlic, herbs and spinach; cook 5 minutes. Season with pepper. Set aside. In medium bowl combine ricotta and Parmesan cheeses, eggs and parsley. Season with nutmeg and pepper.

In 10 x 6 x 3" baking dish spread 1 cup Fresh Tomato-Basil Sauce. Layer with ½ noodles, ½ ricotta-cheese mix and all of spinach-onion mix. Repeat; in final layer use remaining noodles, ricotta-cheese mix and Tomato Sauce. Sprinkle with mozzarella. Bake covered one hour; remove cover and continue baking until bubbly and golden, about 15 minutes.

Makes 8 servings of 265 calories each.

*See note page 101.

Zucchini Stuffed with Spinach, Ricotta and Parmesan, Served with Fresh Tomato-Basil Sauce

6	medium zucchinis (about 3 lbs)
1 tsp	garlic powder
	black pepper, freshly ground, to taste
2 Tbsp	fresh thyme, chopped

Filling:

3 Tbsp	White Vegetable Stock (page 18)
1	large shallot, minced
1	garlic clove, minced
	black pepper, freshly ground, to taste
¼ lb	spinach, chopped
4-5	sun-dried tomatoes,* reconstituted in water, minced
3 Tbsp	fresh basil, chopped, or 1 Tbsp dried
1 cup	nonfat ricotta cheese, or tofu
2 Tbsp	low-fat Parmesan cheese, freshly grated
	black pepper, freshly ground, to taste
2 cups	Fresh Tomato-Basil Sauce (page 32)

Halve zucchinis crosswise. With apple corer, scoop out pulp; leave ¼" intact shells. Season inside shells with garlic powder, pepper and thyme.

In skillet soften shallot, garlic and pepper in Stock. Cook until liquid is absorbed; add spinach, cook till wilted. Transfer to medium bowl. Stir in sun-dried tomatoes, basil, ricotta, Parmesan cheese and pepper. Chill mixture. (Filling can be made 1 day in advance.)

Spoon ricotta mixture into a piping bag fitted with a tip. Pipe filling compactly into each zucchini half (can be done up to 8 hours in advance). Steam zucchinis 4 minutes, or until tender but crisp. Trim and discard ends. Cut stuffed zucchini shells diagonally into 1" slices. Spread ⅓ cup Tomato-Basil Sauce on each plate; decoratively add about 8 zucchini slices.

Serve with ½ cup each brown rice and braised lentils.

Makes 6 servings of 174 calories each. (With rice and lentils, 334 calories each.)

*See note page 102.

Wild rice with dried cherries and scallions.

Grains, Rice & Beans

Bulgur-Wheat Mushroom Timbales

3/4 cup   bulgur wheat

1 cup   White Vegetable Stock (page 18), scalded

1/2 tsp   dried thyme, or 1 tsp black pepper, freshly ground

1 tsp   butter

1/4 lb   small mushrooms, thinly sliced

1/2 tsp   garlic, minced

nonstick vegetable spray

fresh thyme sprigs (garnish)

In medium saucepan melt butter. Add mushrooms; cook 2 minutes. Stir in garlic and remove pan from heat. Remove and reserve 4 mushroom slices.

Add to pan bulgur wheat, Stock and seasoning. Cover pan; let stand 10 minutes.

Spray base and sides of 4 4-oz ramekins. Spoon and pack bulgur mixture into ramekins. Cover with foil. Reheat ramekins before serving. To serve rap ramekins upside down against hard surface to loosen bottom. Remove foil and unmold timbales onto 4 plates. Garnish tops with reserved mushroom slices and thyme sprigs.

Makes 4 servings of 59 calories each.

Bulgur-Wheat Salad with Fresh Mint and Parsley

1/4 cup   tomato, diced

1/4 cup   fresh mint, chopped

3 Tbsp   fresh lemon juice

2 tsp   extra virgin olive oil*

1/2 cup   bulgur or cracked wheat

2/3 cup   White Vegetable Stock (page 18) or water

1/4 cup   green onion, chopped

1/4 cup   fresh parsley, chopped

1 tsp   garlic, minced

1/4 tsp   black pepper, freshly ground

1/4 cup   fresh parsley, chopped (garnish)

In small bowl set wheat. Bring Stock to boil; pour over wheat. Cover. Let stand 10-12 minutes or until tender. Drain excess water. In medium bowl toss wheat with remaining ingredients. Garnish each serving with 1 Tbsp parsley.

Makes 6 servings of 109 calories each.

*See note page 101.

Citrus Couscous with Basil and Apricots

		1 tsp	lemon zest*
		1 tsp	lime zest*
1 cup	White Vegetable Stock (page 18)	2 tsp	orange zest*
		¼ cup	basil leaves, chopped
1 cup	couscous	½ cup	dried apricots, chopped

Bring Stock and zests to boil. Stir in couscous. Cover tightly and remove from heat. Let sit 5-8 minutes. Uncover and stir in remaining ingredients.

Makes 4 ½-cup servings of 166 calories each.

*See note page 102.

Four-Grain Pilaf

		½ tsp	fresh thyme, or ¼ tsp dried leaves
1¾ cups	White Vegetable Stock (page 18)		
⅓ cup	onion, sliced	¼ cup	raw short-grain brown rice
1	bay leaf	¼ cup	raw wild rice
¼ tsp	ground nutmeg	¼ cup	raw wheatberries
¼ tsp	salt	¼ cup	raw barley

In medium saucepan combine Stock, onion, bay leaf, nutmeg, salt and thyme. Bring to boil. Stir in grains; simmer over low heat 35-40 minutes until grains are tender.

Makes 4 servings of 150 calories each.

Fragrant Basmati Rice Pilaf

1 cup	brown or white Basmati rice
	black pepper, freshly ground, to taste
2 Tbsp	cilantro, chopped (optional)

1¾ cups White Vegetable Stock (page 18)
1 small onion, chopped

In medium saucepan combine Stock and onion. Bring to boil. Stir in rice and pepper; simmer, covered, over low heat till rice is tender, 40-45 minutes for brown–15 minutes, white. Before serving stir in cilantro.

Note: For colorful contrast, cook ½ cup brown and ½ cup white Basmati rice separately; stir together before serving. (However, be aware of brown rice's advantage over white: 2X the selenium; 3X the magnesium, Vitamin E and fibre.)

Makes 4 ½-cup servings of 134 calories each.

Japanese Rice with Ginger

1 Tbsp	ginger root, minced
1	bay leaf
1½ cups	raw short-grain brown rice
⅓ cup	green onion chopped
2	egg whites, lightly beaten
	green onions, chopped (garnish)

2¾ cups White Vegetable Stock (page 18)
½ cup onion, diced
1 Tbsp low-sodium soy sauce*
½ tsp fresh thyme

In saucepan combine all ingredients but green onions and egg whites. Bring to boil; cook, covered, over low heat 30 minutes, or until rice is tender.

In small nonstick skillet cook egg whites 1 minute each side, over medium heat. Whites should be firm. Turn out onto cutting board; cut into thin strips. Fold into rice. Garnish and serve.

Makes 6 servings of 140 calories each.

*See note page 102.

70

Pearl Barley with Scallions, Parsley and Mushrooms

		nonstick vegetable spray
	½	large onion, sliced thin
	¼ lb	mushrooms, sliced
	2	scallions, minced
	2 Tbsp	fresh parsley, chopped
3½ cups	White Vegetable Stock (page 18)	½ tsp black pepper, freshly ground
1 cup	pearl barley	1 Tbsp balsamic vinegar

Boil Stock. Add barley. Simmer, covered, 30 minutes or until soft.
Heat and spray medium pan. Sauté onion and mushrooms until soft.
Transfer to bowl. Add barley and remaining ingredients.
Makes 6 ½-cup servings of 125 calories each.

Pink Lentils with Spinach

	1	onion, sliced thin
	1	garlic clove, minced
3½ cups	White Vegetable Stock (page 18)	1 tsp ground cumin
		1 tsp ground coriander
1 cup	pink, green or brown lentils	1 tsp fresh lemon juice
		2 Tbsp sherry wine vinegar
1 tsp	olive oil*	2 lbs spinach

In saucepan bring Stock to boil, add lentils. Lower heat and simmer 20 minutes or until soft.

In medium pan heat oil; add onion, garlic and spices. Cook 2 minutes. Add lemon juice, vinegar and spinach. Cook 3 minutes.

Add lentils to spinach mixture; raise heat and cook 1 minute.

Makes 6 ½-cup servings of 134 calories each.

*See note page 101.

Quinoa with Roasted Sweet Peppers

2 cups	White Vegetable Stock (page 18)
1	orange zest*
1 cup	quinoa**
1	red pepper, roasted, peeled, seeded and chopped
1	yellow pepper, roasted, peeled, seeded and chopped
2 Tbsp	Italian parsley, chopped
½ tsp	black pepper, freshly ground

Boil Stock with orange zest. Add quinoa. Simmer, uncovered, 5 minutes or until soft. Remove from heat. Add remaining ingredients.

Makes 6 ½-cup servings of 92 calories each.

*See note page 102.
**See note page 101.

Wild Rice with Dried Cherries and Scallions

3½ cups	White Vegetable Stock (page 18)
1 cup	wild rice
¼ cup	dried cherries, chopped
3	scallions, minced
1 Tbsp	cilantro, chopped
¼ tsp	black pepper, freshly ground
¼ tsp	jalapeño chile,* minced

Bring Stock and rice to boil, and stir. Reduce heat. Simmer, covered, 40 minutes or until rice is soft. Drain extra liquid. Add remaining ingredients.

Makes 4 ½-cup servings of 170 calories each.

*See note page 101.

Edmond Szekely
1950

Walnut-stuffed cabbage rolls.

Vegetables & Condiments

Apple-Apricot Chutney

1	medium red apple, quartered and cored; grated	
1	medium pear, quartered and cored; grated	

3 Tbsp red bell pepper, minced
15 dried unsweetened apricots (about ¾ cup), finely chopped
3 Tbsp raisins, finely chopped
1 tsp orange zest,* grated
1 tsp apple-cider vinegar
1 tsp honey

Combine all ingredients and stir well.
Makes 1⅓ cups chutney. 1 Tbsp = 24 calories,
*See note page 102.

Artichokes with Hummus Sauce

Hummus Sauce (makes 1¼ cups):
¾ cup   chickpeas, cooked
1   garlic clove, minced
2 Tbsp   tahini or sesame butter
¼ cup   soft tofu
3 Tbsp   fresh lemon juice
½ cup   liquid from cooked or canned chickpeas
1 Tbsp   fresh parsley, chopped
¼ cup   scallions, minced

pinch   black pepper, freshly ground
pinch   cayenne pepper
pinch   salt
4   medium artichokes, leaves and stems trimmed
2   garlic cloves, crushed
1   lemon, juiced
1 tsp   dried oregano
1   bay leaf
4 qt   water
    cherry tomatoes (garnish)
    lettuce leaves (garnish)

In food processor combine chickpeas, garlic clove, tahini, tofu, lemon juice and chickpea liquid. Process until smooth. Transfer to bowl; stir in parsley, scallions, black and cayenne pepper and salt. Serve in decorative bowls.

Cut 1″ off top of artichokes. In large pot combine crushed garlic, lemon, oregano, bay leaf and water. Bring to boil; add artichokes. Boil, covered, 30-35 minutes or until artichoke can be pierced with knife. Remove artichokes and run under cold water. Drain upside down and towel dry. Chill before serving.

Place artichokes on platter. Garnish. Serve with Hummus Sauce.
Artichokes make 4 servings of 15 calories each.
Hummus Sauce, 2 Tbsp = 109 calories.

Corn Relish

6 large corn ears, boiled, kernels removed

½ red onion, in small cubes

1 red bell pepper, in small cubes

1 green bell pepper, in small cubes

1 tomato, cubed

¼ cup cider vinegar

1 tsp black pepper, freshly ground

2 Tbsp cilantro, chopped

¼ tsp dried chili flakes

Combine corn kernels with other ingredients. Refrigerate 2 hours.
Makes 6 servings of 33 calories each.

Fresh Squash Blossoms Filled with Fromage Blanc, Served with Yellow Pepper Sauce

8-10 baby squash (about 3" long) with blossoms attached

2 Tbsp White Vegetable Stock (page 18)

1 Tbsp white wine or vinegar

1 large shallot, minced

1 Tbsp nonfat plain yogurt, smoothed

½ cup low-fat ricotta cheese

1 egg white

1 Tbsp thyme leaves, chopped

pinch ground nutmeg

black pepper, freshly ground, to taste

Rinse squash, leaving blossoms intact. Make 2 lengthwise cuts through squash, beginning about ¼" below blossom. Carefully remove stamen from inside blossom.

In small saucepan soften shallot in Stock and wine over low heat 2 minutes or till liquid evaporates. Cool.

In bowl combine yogurt, ricotta, egg white, thyme and sautéed shallot. Season with nutmeg and pepper. Chill mixture 1 hour. (Filling can be made 1 day in advance.)

Spoon about 1 Tbsp filling into each blossom. Twist ends so filling does not leak out. Steam squashes 3-4 minutes, until tender and blossoms inflated.

Serve with Yellow Pepper Sauce (page 35).

Makes 4 servings of 115 calories each.

Grilled Zucchini with Cilantro Raita

¼ tsp   paprika
2 tsp   cilantro, chopped
1 tsp   fresh mint, chopped
½ tsp   fresh lemon juice
2 tsp   green onion, minced
½ lb   yellow or green zucchini
         (about 2 medium)
1 tsp   corn oil

Cilantro Raita:
1 cup   low-fat plain yogurt
½ tsp   ground cumin

In food processor or blender combine all raita ingredients. Set aside.

Halve zucchini crosswise. Cut each piece in half lengthwise. Brush cut side of zucchini with oil; grill until slightly tender. Serve on decorative platter.

Makes 4 servings of 52 calories each.

Oriental Asparagus

¼ cup   low-sodium soy sauce*
1 Tbsp   Hoisen sauce**
2 Tbsp   cilantro, chopped
2 Tbsp   mango chutney
1 tsp   ginger root, minced
1   garlic clove, minced
¼ tsp   dried chili flakes
1 lb   asparagus, steamed

In blender combine all ingredients but last and process 1 minute. Serve over hot or cold asparagus.

Makes 4 servings of 37 calories each.

*See note page 102.

**Available in Oriental markets.

Roasted Beets with Garlic and Thyme

		8	garlic cloves, peeled
8	medium red beets	2 Tbsp	thyme, chopped
1½ cups	White Vegetable Stock (page 18)	1 Tbsp	black pepper, freshly ground

In ovenproof pan roast all ingredients, covered, at 350°, for 1½ hours or until soft.

Carefully remove skins with paring knife. Serve with garlic cloves.

Makes 4 servings of 61 calories each.

Roasted Red Potatoes with Vinegar

		2 Tbsp	balsamic vinegar
		¾ cup	White Vegetable Stock (page 18)
		1 Tbsp	thyme leaves, chopped
		1 Tbsp	rosemary, chopped
1½ lbs	small red potatoes	1 tsp	black pepper, freshly ground
8	shallots, peeled		

Preheat oven to 350°. Combine all ingredients in ovenproof pan. Roast, covered, 30 minutes. Uncover and cook until soft. Remove potatoes.

On stovetop reduce liquid to form a glaze for potatoes.

Makes 6 servings of 135 calories each.

Spicy Green and Yellow Beans

		½	jalapeño chile,* minced
		¼ tsp	dried chili flakes
		2 Tbsp	sherry wine vinegar
1 lb	yellow and green beans	2	tomatoes, cubed
1½ cups	White Vegetable Stock (page 18)	2 Tbsp	fresh basil, chopped (garnish)

In saucepan place all ingredients but basil. Bring to quick boil. Reducing to simmer, cook 5-8 minutes till beans are crispy and done. Remove beans and set aside.

Reduce liquid to syrup. Pour over beans. Garnish and serve.

Makes 4 servings of 58 calories each.

*See note page 101.

Walnut-Stuffed Cabbage Rolls

		2	small green onions, cut in 2″ julienne
1	Chinese (Napa) or savoy cabbage head (about 1 lb)	1¼ cups	walnuts, freshly chopped
½ lb	fresh spinach	⅛ tsp	sansho pepper or freshly ground black pepper
1 Tbsp	canola oil		
1 tsp	fresh garlic, minced		
1	small carrot, cut in 2″ julienne	1½ Tbsp	low-sodium soy sauce*
1	small zucchini, cut in 2″ julienne	½ cup	White Vegetable Stock (page 18)
1	small celery stalk, cut in 2″ julienne	2 Tbsp	potato starch, dissolved in 4 Tbsp water
		1 cup	bean sprouts

Remove 4 large outer leaves from cabbage, and blanch in boiling water until barely wilted (about 4 minutes). Remove from water and cool. Shred about 2 cups of remaining cabbage; set aside.

Trim spinach. Cut small root off base of each bunch to hold leaves together. Place in skillet; add water to cover. Bring to boil to blanch briefly. Remove from heat, drain and cool.

In wok or heavy skillet heat oil. Sauté garlic; add carrot, celery, zucchini and green onions. Mix quickly. Add shredded cabbage; mix again. Stir in walnuts and pepper. Add drained spinach, soy sauce and Stock. Bring to boil; add potato starch. Stir gently till mixture thickens. Add bean sprouts. Do not overcook—vegetables should be crisp. Remove from heat.

Preheat oven to 350°.

Divide vegetables among 4 blanched cabbage leaves. Roll up leaves lengthwise to enclose vegetables. Place, folded side down, in skillet. Pour any remaining sauce over all. Reheat gently to serve.

Makes 4 servings of 151 calories each.

*See note page 102.

Persian pancakes with cinnamon-cheese filling.

Breakfast, Brunch & Baked Goods

Banana-Bran Muffins

1½ cups	unprocessed bran*
½ cup	apple juice
1	egg
3 Tbsp	canola oil
⅓ cup	honey
¼ cup	low-fat buttermilk

1⅓ cups	whole-wheat flour**
1¼ tsp	baking soda, sifted
¼ tsp	salt
½ tsp	ground cinnamon
¼ tsp	ground cloves
1	ripe banana, diced, or ¾ cup fresh (or unthawed frozen) blueberries

Preheat oven to 350°. Line 14-16 muffin-pan cups (2½" diameter) with paper muffin cups.

In medium bowl combine bran and apple juice. Let sit 8 minutes. In large bowl whisk together egg, oil, honey and buttermilk.

In another medium bowl combine flour, soda, salt and spices; use fork to mix.

With only 10-15 strokes stir flour and bran mixtures into liquids. Fold in bananas until just combined. Do not overmix.

Using a ¼-cup dry measure, scoop mixture into muffin cups (they will be about ⅔ full).

Bake 20-25 minutes, or until muffins spring back when pressed. Remove muffins from tins. Cool completely on cooling rack.

(Muffins can be frozen. To serve: defrost; reheat by placing in foil and baking 15-20 minutes at 350°.)

Makes approximately 15 muffins of 117 calories each.

*See note page 101.

**See note page 102.

Blueberry-Bran Muffins

1 cup	Miller's wheat-bran flakes*
¼ cup	unprocessed oat bran*
1 cup	whole-wheat flour**
1 tsp	baking soda
1¼ tsp	ground cinnamon

1 cup	low-fat buttermilk
¾ cup	ripe banana (1 large), mashed
¼ cup	wild-sage honey
1	large egg
1 cup	blueberries, fresh, or frozen (thawed); or fresh raspberries, chopped

Preheat oven to 375.° Line with paper muffin cups 16 regular-size (2½" across top) muffin cups.

In medium bowl stir brans, flour, soda and spices. In large bowl whisk buttermilk, banana, honey, and egg until smooth. Add flour mix to liquid mix; stir until dry ingredients are moistened; fold in berries. Half-fill muffin cups with batter. Bake 25 minutes, or until muffins spring back when pressed in center. Turn onto cooling rack.

Makes 16 muffins of 78 calories each.

These freeze well. To serve, defrost and reheat 15 minutes at 350.°

*See note page 101.

**See note page 102.

85

Fresh Corncakes

¼ cup yellow cornmeal
1 cup low-fat milk
1 egg, separated
⅔ cup fresh corn kernels
2 Tbsp green onion, minced
1 tsp fresh oregano, minced, or
       ¼ tsp dried, crumbled

black pepper, freshly grated, to taste
nonstick vegetable spray
⅔ cup low-fat cheese (such as Gouda or mozzarella), freshly grated
fresh oregano (garnish)

In small saucepan combine milk and cornmeal. Cook about 5 minutes over low heat, stirring constantly until thickened. Remove and cool.

Transfer mixture to medium bowl. Stir in egg yolk, corn, onion, 1 tsp oregano, and pepper.

Beat egg white until stiff. Fold ¼ into corn mixture. Then fold in remainder.

Heat large nonstick skillet over low heat; spray. Add corn mixture by heaping tablespoonful. Do not crowd pan. Sauté and turn over cakes until cooked in center and browned, about 4-5 minutes. Remove. Spray lightly for each remaining batter batch.

Before serving sprinkle each cake with about 2 tsp cheese. Garnish.

Makes 16 small cakes of 35 calories each.

Grapefruit Gazpacho

2 medium tomatoes, peeled, seeded and finely chopped
1 cup cucumber, peeled and grated

½ cup celery, finely chopped
½ cup bell pepper, finely chopped
2 Tbsp fresh parsley, chopped
1½ cups fresh grapefruit juice
fructose (optional), to taste
parsley sprigs (garnish)

If grapefruit juice is slightly tart, adjust with a little fructose.

Combine all ingredients by hand, or mix in blender on pulse cycle. Chill well (at least 2 hours). Garnish and serve.

Makes 4 servings of 66 calories each.

Muesli

¾ cup   rolled oats (old-fashioned variety)

6   sun-dried black mission figs, chopped

¼ tsp   ground cinnamon
⅔ cup   water
½   medium apple, with skin
1   banana, sliced
1 cup   low-fat plain yogurt
8   almonds or hazelnuts

Combine oats, figs and cinnamon; cover with water and soak overnight.

Before serving, grate apple and stir into oat mixture. Divide in 4 portions; trim each with banana slices; top with ¼ cup yogurt sprinkled with nuts.

(Note: Other sun-dried fruit such as apricots, dates or prunes may be substituted for figs.)

Makes 4 servings of 202 calories each.

Persian Pancakes

2   eggs
½ tsp   canola oil

¼ tsp   ground nutmeg
¼ tsp   ground cinnamon
½ cup   whole-wheat flour*
1 cup   nonfat milk
  nonstick vegetable spray

In bowl combine eggs, oil, cinnamon and nutmeg. Add flour to make paste. Whisk in milk, blending well. Refrigerate 2 hours. Heat and spray small nonstick pan. Pour in 1/12 of crêpe batter, circling to coat pan bottom. Cook 1 minute, each side. Remove and fill with Cinnamon-Cheese Filling. Repeat.

Makes 12 crêpes of 34 calories each, without filling.
Makes 12 crêpes of 60 calories each, with filling.

*See note page 102.

Cinnamon-Cheese Filling

12 oz   nonfat cottage cheese
1 Tbsp   ground cinnamon

1 tsp   ground nutmeg
1 Tbsp   fructose or sugar
½ cup   golden raisins (optional)

Combine all ingredients. Set to rest in refrigerator 1½ hours. Place 1 oz filling in each crêpe. Serve with fresh fruit.

Makes 12 1-oz servings of 27 calories each, without raisins.

Tecate Ranch Whole-Wheat Bread

3 cups	warm water 105-110°	8½-9½ cups	stone-ground whole-wheat flour*
¼ cup	wild-sage honey	1 cup	Miller's wheat-bran flakes**
1 packet	active dry yeast (¼ oz)	2 Tbsp plus 1 tsp	poppy or sesame seeds
½ cup	cold-pressed safflower or sunflower oil	1½ tsp	sea salt
		1	egg white, beaten (for glaze)

In medium bowl combine water and honey. Sprinkle over yeast; stir to dissolve. Let stand 5 minutes or until frothy. Stir in oil if preparing dough by hand; knead thoroughly to ensure lightness and as much gluten as possible.

In electric-mixer bowl or large bowl, combine yeast mix with oil, 8½ cups flour, bran, 2 Tbsp seeds and salt. Knead dough in electric mixer fitted with dough hook. (Or knead by hand about 10 minutes on work surface.) If dough is very sticky, add ¼ cup flour at a time; continue to knead 10-15 minutes or until dough pulls away from sides of mixing bowl and is smooth and elastic.

Shape dough into ball. Lightly brush large bowl with vegetable oil. Add dough, turning to coat surface. Cover with damp kitchen towel; let dough rise about 1 hour until volume doubles.

Brush lightly with oil 2 9x5x2″ loaf pans. Punch down dough; divide in half. Knead until smooth. Shape into loaf pans. Make ⅛″ lengthwise slash on each loaf. Let rise about 45 minutes until volume doubles. Brush tops with beaten egg white; sprinkle with remaining seeds. Preheat oven to 350°.

Bake 35-40 minutes or until loaves sound hollow and are golden brown on top. Remove from pans. Cool completely on racks before slicing.

Makes 2 loaves, or 50 ½-inch slices of 107 calories each.

To freeze, wrap sliced loaves in plastic bags and keep up to 2 months.

*See note page 102.

**See note page 101.

Zucchini-Spinach Frittata

		2	eggs
		4	egg whites
3 cups	zucchini	¼ cup	low-fat milk
1 Tbsp	vegetable seasoning	2 tsp	fresh garlic, minced
¾ cup	fresh spinach, cooked, squeezed, and chopped	1	medium onion, diced
		1 tsp	dried whole thyme
1 tsp	dried sweet basil	2 Tbsp	White Vegetable Stock (page 18)
1 Tbsp	Parmesan or Romano cheese, freshly grated		
		1 cup	raw mushrooms, thickly sliced
½ tsp	black pepper, freshly ground		
		½ cup	artichoke hearts, thickly sliced
2 Tbsp	chives or green onions, coarsely chopped		
		3 oz	mozzarella cheese, sliced

Preheat oven to 350°.

In large bowl grate zucchini. Add vegetable seasoning and mix well. Let stand in colander about ½ hour. Combine with spinach. Add basil, grated cheese, pepper and chives. Mix well.

In separate bowl beat eggs, egg whites and milk. Combine with zucchini mixture.

In 9″ skillet gently sauté garlic, onion and thyme in Stock until starting to soften. Add mushrooms; stir with wooden spoon till they start to soften. Add artichokes; heat well.

Transfer mixture to casserole. Pour spinach/zucchini mixture over onion mixture. Let bubble a few seconds. Cover with sliced cheese. Bake 45-50 minutes, till knife comes out clean when tested.

Remove from oven and let sit 10 minutes.

Makes 6 servings of 110 calories each.

Fresh berry pudding.

Desserts & Sweet Sauces

Apple-Pear Butter with Cinnamon and Orange Zest

Sweet and spicy with Tecate Ranch Whole-Wheat Bread (page 88) and muffins.

½ lb	pears (1 medium), cored and chopped
½ lb	tart apples (about 1 medium), peeled, cored and chopped
¾ cup	unsweetened apple or pear juice
½ tsp	vanilla extract
¼ tsp	ground cinnamon
⅛ tsp	ground nutmeg
1 tsp	orange zest, minced*

In medium non-aluminum pot combine all ingredients. Bring to boil; cook, covered, over low heat until softened, about 25 minutes. In blender or food processor purée until smooth. Cover and refrigerate.

Makes about 1½ cups, or 12 2-Tbsp servings of 22 calories each.

Can be refrigerated up to 5 days.

*See note page 102.

Carob-Raspberry Mousse

1 Tbsp	unflavored gelatin		¼ cup	granulated fructose or sugar
2 Tbsp	cold water		4 Tbsp	carob powder
¼ cup	unsweetened apple juice		1 tsp	vanilla extract
⅓ cup	raspberries (fresh or frozen), puréed and strained		1 cup	low-fat ricotta cheese
			1¼ cup	non-fat plain yogurt

In small bowl place gelatin; pour over water. Let stand 5 minutes.

In small pot combine apple juice, raspberry purée and fructose. Bring to boil over low heat; whisk in gelatin and carob powder until smooth; add vanilla. Cool.

In blender combine carob mixture, ricotta and yogurt. Process until smooth.

Pour into 4 ramekins. Let stand at room temperature 2 hours before serving. Or refrigerate after 1 hour but let drop to room temperature before serving.

Makes 4-5 large ramekins of 238 calories each.

Creamy Cinnamon Flan

			1	large egg
⅔ cup	low-fat milk		1½ Tbsp	wild-sage honey
3 Tbsp	low-fat ricotta cheese		1 tsp	vanilla extract
			¼ tsp	ground cinnamon, plus sprinkle

Preheat oven to 350.° Lightly brush with vegetable oil 4 ½-cup baking dishes.

Combine all ingredients in blender or food processor until smooth. In medium baking pan set 4 baking dishes ¾ full of custard; half-fill pan with water. Bake 30 minutes or until flan centers are just set. Remove flans from pan. Before serving, sprinkle with dash of cinnamon.

Makes 4 servings of 94 calories each.

Fresh Berry Pudding

¼ cup	orange juice, freshly squeezed	1 cup	fresh strawberries, hulled and quartered*
1 tsp	vanilla extract	1 cup	fresh raspberries*
½ cup	fresh blueberries*	½ cup	non-fat plain yogurt
		1	small banana, mashed
		6	mint sprigs (garnish)

In medium bowl combine juice, vanilla and berries. Toss gently. Let sit 10 minutes. Stir yogurt with banana until smooth. Fold yogurt mix into berries. Spoon pudding into 6 dessert bowls or stemmed glasses. Garnish. Serve chilled.

Makes about 6 ⅔-cup servings of 59 calories each.

*You can substitute frozen unsweetened berries (thawed) for fresh.

Fresh Fruit in Orange Cup with Amaretto Sauce

		3 Tbsp	amaretto liqueur
		¼ cup	fresh orange juice
		1	red delicious apple, cored and diced
		½ cup	melon, diced
		½ cup	pineapple, diced
2	oranges	8	strawberries, sliced
12	whole almonds toasted	½ cup	grapes

Halve oranges crosswise. Scoop out pulp to form cups. Reserve pulp for sauce. Set cups aside.

Combine in blender orange pulp, almonds, amaretto and juice. Blend till very smooth.

In medium bowl combine fruit. Divide into orange cups. Top each cup with sauce.

Makes 4 servings of 110 calories each.

Frozen Fruit Sorbet

2 cups fresh seasonal fruit such as melon, plums, nectarines, bananas, berries, papaya, mango, pineapple or combination thereof, peeled and diced in 1″ pcs.

In large freeze-proof dish arrange fruit in 1 layer. Freeze until fruit is partially frozen very firm, about 1-1½ hours. Put 1 cup fruit in food-processor bowl; process until slightly chunky. Transfer to medium bowl; reserve. Process remaining fruit until slightly chunky; add reserved fruit; process until smooth; do not allow to defrost completely.

For a creamier sorbet, frozen fruit can be processed through a Champion Juicer, available at natural food stores.

Spoon ½ cup sorbet each into 4 chilled dessert dishes; set in freezer 20-30 minutes before serving.

For a decorative presentation, spoon sorbet into pastry bag fitted with wide-star tip; pipe into dessert dishes.

Makes 4 servings of 44 calories each.

Melon Fan with Strawberry Purée

1 medium honeydew or cantaloupe (about 3 lbs)

1 pt fresh strawberries, hulled and sliced (reserve 12 slices for garnish)

⅛ tsp ground nutmeg

1 tsp fresh mint, chopped

4 mint sprigs (garnish)

Halve melon lengthwise and remove seeds. Cut each half into 3 wedges. With small knife cut away peel, leaving melon wedges intact. Starting 1″ from end, cut each melon wedge so there are 4 slices. Spread slices to resemble fan.

In blender or food processor combine berries, nutmeg and chopped mint, and purée until smooth.

Place 2 Tbsp sauce on each of 6 plates, set melon fan on sauce and garnish.

Makes 6 servings of 44 calories each.

Poached Pears
with Cassis

2 large Bartlett pears, peeled, halved lengthwise and cored

1 cup unsweetened cranberry juice*

½ cup water

¼ cup Crème de Cassis liqueur

1 Tbsp fresh lemon juice

1 cinnamon stick

6 whole cloves

4 mint sprigs (garnish)

In medium saucepan combine Cassis, juices, spices and water. Bring to boil; add pears and simmer, uncovered, over low heat 8-10 minutes.

Remove pears with slotted spoon. Reduce liquid to ½ cup. Sauce should have consistency of syrup. Chill sauce and 4 plates until serving. On each plate pour ¼ sauce; in center place pear half, core side down. Garnish with mint.

Makes 4 servings of 138 calories each.

*Available at natural-foods stores.

Ricotta Cheesecake with Ginger

		1 packet	unflavored gelatin (¼ oz)
		¾ cup	apple juice
		1 cup	low-fat ricotta cheese
1 cup	Grape Nuts cereal	⅔ cup	non-fat plain yogurt
2 Tbsp	sweet butter, melted, or vegetable oil	⅛ tsp	ground ginger
		¼ tsp	ground nutmeg
1 Tbsp	apple juice	½ cup	whole or sliced strawberries
2 Tbsp	cold water		

Preheat oven to 350.° Brush with vegetable oil sides and base of 9″ tart pan with removable bottom. In food processor crumble Grape Nuts until fine; add butter and 1 Tbsp juice; blend until crumbs are moist. With moist fingers pat crumbs into base of tart pan. Bake 8 minutes. Cool.

In medium bowl dissolve gelatin in water. Bring ¾ cup juice to boil; whisk into gelatin. In food processor combine gelatin mix, cheese, yogurt and ginger until very smooth. Pour into crust. Sprinkle with nutmeg. Chill 2 hours or overnight. Serve each cheesecake slice with 4-5 berries.

Makes 12 servings of 101 calories each.

Strawberries with Kahlúa Crème

		1 Tbsp	honey or apple juice concentrate
		2 tsp	Kahlúa liqueur
		1 tsp	vanilla extract
2 Tbsp	low-fat milk	1 pt	fresh strawberries, hulled; halved if small, quartered if large
½ cup	low-fat ricotta cheese		

In blender or food processor combine milk, cheese, honey, Kahlúa and vanilla, and process until very smooth. Spoon sauce on each of 4 plates. Add berries.

Makes 4 servings of 97 calories each.

Strawberry Sauce

With Vanilla-Yogurt Sauce (page 99) a fine accompaniment to Seasonal Fresh Fruit Salad (page 24)

1½ cups whole fresh strawberries, rinsed and hulled (or frozen unsweetened strawberries, thawed)

1 medium banana, cut in 1" pcs

¼ cup unsweetened apple juice

1 tsp fresh lemon juice

In food processor or blender combine all ingredients until smooth. Cover and refrigerate up to 4 days.

Makes about 1¼ cups, or 10 2-Tbsp servings of 32 calories each.

Sweet-Potato Soufflé with Orange and Toasted Pecans

½ lb sweet potatoes (or yams), peeled and cut in ¼" slices

¾ cup orange juice, freshly squeezed

1 cup water

1½ Tbsp wild-sage honey

1 tsp vanilla extract

1 Tbsp orange zest,* grated

1 tsp crystallized ginger, grated

½ tsp ground cinnamon

⅛ tsp ground nutmeg

2 large egg whites

¼ tsp cream of tartar

4 tsp pecans, toasted and chopped (garnish)

Preheat oven to 400.° Lightly brush with vegetable oil 4 ½-cup soufflé dishes or 1 3-cup soufflé dish about 6" diameter x 4" depth.

In medium saucepan cook, covered, juice, water and sweet potatoes until very soft, about 40-45 minutes. (If liquid evaporates before potatoes are cooked, add ¼ cup water and cook until potatoes are soft.) Drain any liquid from pan. In blender or food processor purée potatoes, honey, vanilla, zest and spices. With electric mixer, beat egg whites with cream of tartar until stiff but not dry. Fold ½ of whites into potato mix; then gently fold in remainder. Fill individual soufflé dishes ¾ full or spoon into 3-cup soufflé dish. Bake: individual soufflés, 16-18 minutes; 3-cup soufflé, 25 minutes—or until soufflés are slightly puffy and golden. Garnish. Serve immediately.

Makes 4 servings of 112 calories each.

*See note page 102.

Vanilla-Yogurt Sauce

With Strawberry Sauce (page 98), a fine accompaniment to Seasonal Fresh Fruit Salad (page 24).

1	medium banana, cut in 1″ pcs.
½ cup	non-fat plain yogurt
¼ cup	unsweetened apple juice
1 tsp	vanilla extract

In blender or bowl of food processor combine all ingredients until smooth.

Makes about 1¼ cups, or 10 2-Tbsp servings of 23 calories each.

Warm Apple Crisp with Crunchy Granola Topping

½ cup	unsweetened apple juice
⅛ tsp	ground cinnamon
pinch	ground nutmeg
4 Tbsp	Old-Time Granola or plain or flavored packaged granola without brown sugar or saturated fats
2	large tart green apples (about ¾ lb), cored, sliced ¼" thick

Preheat oven to 375°. In 4 1-cup baking dishes place apple slices, skin side up. Over them divide apple juice, cinnamon and nutmeg. Set dishes on large baking sheet, cover with foil, bake 30 minutes. Uncover; divide granola over each serving. Bake, uncovered, 5 minutes. Serve warm.

Makes 4 servings of 112 calories each.

Old-Time Granola

3 Tbsp	wild-sage honey
1 Tbsp	cold-pressed safflower oil
2 cups	old-fashioned rolled oats
½ cup	apple juice
¼ cup	unbleached raw almonds or hazelnuts, chopped
½ tsp	orange zest
¼ cup	raw sunflower seeds
2 tsp	vanilla extract
¼ cup	raw wheat germ
1 tsp	ground cinnamon
2 Tbsp	whole-wheat flour
½ tsp	ground coriander
	¼ tsp	ground nutmeg

Preheat oven to 250°. In large bowl toss together all ingredients until well mixed.

Spread in thin layer on baking sheet. Bake, stirring often (for even browning) until light brown, about 20-25 minutes.

Let cool on sheet. Transfer to covered container.

Keeps, at room temperature, up to 2 weeks.

Recipe Notes

Bran, Miller's. Some package labels call it Miller's Bran; others, Natural Unprocessed Bran Flakes. Wheat or oat, it's always on view in health-food stores. Now many supermarkets stock a section with 100 percent natural products such as this.

Chiles, Ancho. Hispanic or gourmet specialty markets carry this robust capsicum. If unavailable, substitute green chiles like the California or Pasilla, which can be found in cans at the market. Remember that the little seeds as well as the veins in the chiles represent a lot of concentrated heat. Remove them if you're not into fiery Mexican cuisine.

Chiles, Jalapeño. Although the jalapeño is not at the top of the chile thermostat, when chopped it is a serious skin irritant. To do your chopping, cover your hands with plastic gloves or a plastic bag. Watch the inclusion of seeds and veins as you must with any chile variety.

Chiles, Serrano. Many recipes use jalapeños and serranos interchangeably. However, the serrano is more than a tad hotter. And watch those seeds and veins in preparation.

Chiles, Whole, Roasted. For recipe testing, we used the Ortega brand, which does not identify the green chiles that the can calls Whole Roasted. However, they are obviously either California or Anaheim. Don't forget to remove the seeds and veins.

Mustard, Dijon-type. For testing our recipes, we used Grey Poupon. Shop around for low-sodium versions. A Dijon-type mustard can contain as much as 465 milligrams of sodium per tablespoonful.

Olive Oil. Imported Italian is the international choice. There are so many varieties that tasting parties have become popular. Be advised that Lite refers to consistency and flavor. The spectrum ranges from Extra Virgin to Pure; to the educated palate, there's considerable difference. Extra Virgin and Virgin Olive Oil come from the first pressing of the olive and retain a distinct olive flavor. Pure Olive Oil printed on a label indicates a taste not so identifiable (because water has been added and the product has then undergone a second pressing). On any label of any variety, Cold Pressed is always best.

Quinoa. Pronounce it keen-wah. Always rinse this grain very thoroughly before you cook it. A good source of protein, calcium and the amino acid lysine.

Soy Sauce. In our recipe testing we used low-sodium Westbrae Natural Soy Sauce. It contains only 155 salt milligrams per teaspoon. The usual count is 350 or so.

Tomatillos. These resemble green tomatoes and have a tart lemony flavor. They are fairly common in the gourmet-produce corner of large supermarkets. When canned, they're called Mexican Tomatoes.

Tomatoes, Sun-Dried. Buy them in gourmet-food stores or Italian markets. Carefully rinse away their oil (unwanted and unnecessary calories).

Whole-Wheat Flour, Stone-Ground. Like Miller's Bran, this has always been a staple at health-food stores, but you might find it in a well-supplied supermarket.

Worcestershire Sauce. A low-sodium version contains 57 sodium milligrams per tablespoonful, as against 147.

Zest. The thin outer peel of citrus fruit, with all white membranes cut and scraped away.

Cooks, Chefs, Cocineros y Cocineras

Rancho La Puerta's cooks and cookery are an inextricable part of the Ranch success story.

Preceding them all, of course, was my mother's own kitchen. Many of our first Ranch dishes were based on our family recipes. Mother spent a number of years helping us work out and continually improve a selective, healthful diet of natural foods.

My husband contributed guidance. He also searched out unexpected sources for foods we did not process ourselves. In Alhambra, California he discovered a genuine old-fashioned Dutch miller purveying natural grains. From the Pasteur Institute in Paris he imported a culture he considered superior to yogurt—acidophilus (ancestor to much of the present-day acidophilus in America because we gave away many "starter sets"). At first we dried all our own fruit on chicken-wire racks spread out in the sun, till the Professor located a Coachella Valley rancher who specialized in nonsulfured dates.

The two oldest recipes in this book evolved from Edmond Szekely's deep concern about nutrition. Our whole-grain wheat bread has had many names. For a time we called it Zarathustra Bread because it was suggested by my husband's Zoroastrian research.

Our Ranch version of this unleavened bread from the Persian empire of more than a thousand years ago we baked in a primitive outdoor oven common in Mexico for centuries. Whenever old friends reminisce about early days at Rancho La Puerta, they nostalgically recall the tantalizing aroma when hot loaves were laboriously pulled from that round brick oven. The perfume quickly permeated the Ranch, drawing a crowd eager for organic honey on hot bread.

After many phases, Ranch bread is now simplified (page 88), lighter in weight (if an early unleavened loaf had been thrown in anger, it would have constituted a lethal weapon) and still a breakfast favorite at both the Ranch and the Golden Door.

Another coup of 50 years ago was our introduction of what was then regarded as a bit of exotica—muesli (page 87). Our muesli recipe derived from the original attributed to the esteemed Bircher-Benner Clinic in

103

Switzerland. Now muesli is indeed a household word, printed on millions of commercialized-cereal boxes.

From time to time a dietician would supervise the kitchen, especially during the era (1950ish) of our two separate dining rooms. The theory behind the Diet Dining Room was that to restrict calories should be easier if one were not exposed to the sight of higher-calorie fare. This cheerful rendezvous, ceiling striped with Mexicana pastels, offered a weekly prize and flourished into the 1960s. Finally we merged the two facilities when it became apparent that all our guests were dieters.

I wish there were space to detail the exuberant year-by-year saga of our culinary history and our experiments with foodstuffs then unheard of in America but being rediscovered today. The three decades of our picturesque grape-arbor Dining Room – with its indoor and outdoor capacity seating and its colorful autumn grape festival – should have a full chapter. And I would enjoy describing the zestful personalities who presided over our kitchen and poured such ardor into their creative work.

But since we are already into the book's last few pages, I will have to make do with grateful mention of the antecedents of the current jefe of the Rancho La Puerta food-services department. Their lasting influence is apparent throughout this book. Their best memorial, the Ranch dining tradition, which our guests so appreciate and for which we feel such pride and affection:

Margarita Arellano (30 years), Carlos Badillo, Joel Brown, Sam Demetrius (5 years), Inéz Hernández (30 years), Daisy Klein, Maybella Koberg (15 years), Adela Loya (20 years), Carlos Munoz, Juan Muruato, Felipe Olmos, María Rivera (35 years) and Caroline Wilson.

I close with a tribute to Chef Bill Wavrin, Sous Chef Rigoberto Ramirez Pacheco, and to Michel Stroot, Executive Chef at the Golden Door. Our legacy is safe in their good hands. The hundreds of letters from guests requesting recipes reflect the chefs' enthusiasm and commitment.

This final paragraph is written with a genuine sense of a promise fulfilled. It is now for you to take heed and begin to live the younger/longer life.

D.S.

Index and Nutrition Charts

Nutritional analysis,
recipe by recipe

Note: A milligram equals 1/1000 of a gram.
A gram equals about 1/28 of an ounce.

Page No.	Recipe	Calories	Protein grams	Carbo-hydrates grams	Fat grams	Cholesterol milligrams	Sodium mg.
30	Ancho Chile Sauce	30	1	4	0.2	3	36
76	Apple-Apricot Chutney	24	0.3	6.1	0.1	0	1
92	Apple-Pear Butter	22	1	6	0.1	0	1
76	Artichokes with Hummus Sauce	109	4.8	16.1	3.5	0	37
30	Avocado Sauce with Lemon and Fresh Herbs	25	1	3	0.1	0	14
52	Baked Eggplant Gratin with Ricotta Soufflé	130	8.5	13.4	3.8	46	143
38	Baked Pasta Casserole	255	13	44	4.3	9	159
53	Baked Sea Bass in Romaine with California Salsa	165	21.1	6.3	5.5	100	80
31	Balsamic Vinaigrette	75	1	7	5.1	0	6
84	Banana-Bran Muffins	117	2.8	18.5	3.8	18	110
54	Black Bean Flauta with Two Sauces	187	9	33	2.8	2	283
14	Black Bean Soup with Cumin and Tomatoes	116	6	21	1.7	0	115
85	Blueberry-Bran Muffins	78	2	16	0.9	19	52
68	Bulgur-Wheat Mushroom Timbales	59	1.6	10.4	1.4	3	2
68	Bulgur-Wheat Salad with Fresh Mint and Parsley	109	2	20	2.6	0	6
22	Cabbage Salad with Bleu Cheese, Apples and Walnuts	95	2	15	4.0	1	56
93	Carob Raspberry Mousse	238	13	37	5.8	23	153
15	Carrot Bisque with Curry	289	6.4	16	2.2	0	109
55	Charbroiled Swordfish with Red Bell Pepper-Saffron Sauce	252	33.2	11.4	7.3	201	132
56	Chiles Rellenos	202	27	32.2	5.2	86	203

Per Serving

15	Chilled Melon Soup	88	2.6	21.2	0.0	0.5	39
16	Chunky Gazpacho with Cucumber	28	1	3	0.2	3	132
69	Citrus Couscous with Basil and Apricots	166	3.3	30	4.1	10	48
39	Cobb Salad	205	12	26	6.7	106	230
77	Corn Relish	33	1.1	7.9	0.3	0	3
93	Creamy Cinnamon Flan	94	5	10	3.8	109	61
31	Creamy Ranch Dressing	25	3	2	0.6	2	80
23	Cucumber and Red Onion Salad with Fresh Dill	32	1	5	1.4	0	4
39	Fettucini Alfredo	239	12.6	38	3.5	52	178
69	Four-Grain Pilaf	150	5.6	28.5	1.5	0.4	1.5
70	Fragrant Basmati-Rice Pilaf	134	4.9	25	1.5	0.4	2.5
94	Fresh Berry Pudding	59	2	13	0.4	0	16
86	Fresh Corncakes	35	2.2	4	1.2	20	29
94	Fresh Fruit in Orange Cup with Amaretto Sauce	116	2.2	23.5	2.4	0	3
32	Fresh Herb-Mustard Vinaigrette	32	1	4	2.4	0	27
77	Fresh Squash Blossoms Filled with Fromage Blanc	115	6.4	14.1	2.9	10	70
32	Fresh Tomato-Basil Sauce	49	2	11	0.5	0	19
95	Frozen Fruit Sorbet	44	1	10	0.5	0	0
23	Garden Harvest Salad	188	22	23	3.0	10	492
86	Grapefruit Gazpacho	60	1.8	15	0.3	0	22
33	Grapefruit Vinaigrette	49	1	7	2.3	0	2
46	Grilled Eggplant and Goat-Cheese Pizza with Thyme	233	9	42	4.6	8	227
78	Grilled Zucchini with Cucumber Raita	52	3.9	6.3	1.3	1	46

Page No.	Recipe	Calories	Protein grams	Carbo-hydrates grams	Fat grams	Cholesterol milligrams	Sodium mg.
16	Hearty Yellow Split-Pea Soup	90	4	15	1.6	0	38
70	Japanese Rice with Ginger	140	6.2	25.2	1.6	0.5	259
57	Layered Tamale Pie with Corn, Tomatoes and Cheese	233	11	42	4.1	7	127
40	Lentil and Mushroom Enchiladas	145	6	25	3.7	3	107
17	Lentil Soup with Swiss Chard and Thyme	71	3	14	1.2	0	84
58	Marinated Tofu "Steaks" with Pineapple Salsa	154	9.9	18.8	5.6	0	29
95	Melon Fan with Strawberry Purée	44	1	10.2	0.4	0	8
59	Mock Swordfish with Ancho Chile Sauce and Spinach	165	13	11	9.5	2	138
87	Muesli	202	7.2	38.7	3.4	1	46
47	Mushroom and Parmesan-Cheese Pizza with Fennel	214	9	41	3.3	1	138
78	Oriental Asparagus	37	3.4	7	0.3	0	263
41	Pasta Primavera with Lemony Pesto	200	8	37	2.9	3	78
71	Pearl Barley with Scallions, Parsley and Mushrooms	125	4.8	42	0.4	0	4
87	Persian Pancakes with Cinnamon-Cheese Filling	60	5.9	7.4	0.7	1.5	142
33	Pesto Sauce with Lemon	92	2	3	8.7	2	47
71	Pink Lentils with Spinach	134	9.8	20	2.2	0	75
34	Piquant Ranch Salsa	22	1	4	0.2	1	253
96	Poached Pears with Cassis	138	0.4	27.7	0.5	0	5
60	Poached Sole with Dill Sauce	251	39.2	14.4	8.4	61	172
18	Potato-Leek Soup with Fresh Sage	94	3	20	0.6	2	22
72	Quinoa with Roasted Sweet Peppers	92	3.3	30	0.6	0	4

108

97	Ricotta Cheesecake with Ginger	101	4.7	12.2	4.0	6.6	102
79	Roasted Beets with Garlic and Thyme	61	1.8	13.7	0.4	0	52
42	Roasted Chile Custard	210	14.6	11.6	12.1	294	530
79	Roasted Red Potatoes with Vinegar	135	4.4	47	0.3	0	16
60	Scampi Provencal	132	15.2	7.2	4.1	112	115
24	Seasonal Fresh Fruit Salad	178	4	42	1.2	1	50
61	Snapper Veracruz	184	31	10	0.4	86	145
80	Spicy Green and Yellow Beans	58	2.9	13.2	0.5	0	10
24	Spinach and Goat-Cheese Salad with Balsamic Vinaigrette	71	3	6	4.3	6	127
43	Spinach-Cheese Quesadillas	125	6	16	5.0	10	133
97	Strawberries with Kahlúa Crème	97	4.2	12.9	2.6	10	44
98	Strawberry Sauce	32	0	8	0.2	0	2
62	Stuffed Baked Potato with Broccoli	165	10	23	3.9	12	235
63	Stuffed Bell Peppers with Bulgur Wheat and Tofu	207	7.9	40	2.5	0.2	115
44	Stuffed Tomato with Tuna Salad	227	35	21	2.0	59	162
98	Sweet Potato Soufflé with Orange and Toasted Pecans	112	4	24	0.3	0	46
88	Tecate Ranch Whole-Wheat Bread	107	2.5	17.9	2.6	0	60
44	Tempeh Reuben Sandwich	149	9.8	22	4.8	27.2	316
25	Tempeh Tostada Salad with Tomatillo Salsa	264	16.2	30.8	9.7	54.4	226
45	Toasted Cheese and Tomato Sandwich	148	5	20	5.3	12	120
34	Tomatillo Salsa with Cilantro	69	2	16	0.3	0	204
47	Tomato and Pesto Pizza	276	12	41	9.2	8	198

Page No.	Recipe	Calories	Protein grams	Carbo-hydrates grams	Fat grams	Cholesterol milligrams	Sodium mg.
99	Vanilla-Yogurt Sauce	23	1	5	0.0	0	9
46	Vegetable Pizza	223	9	41	4.0	4	153
81	Walnut-Stuffed Cabbage Rolls	151	8	23	4.5	0.1	200
100	Warm Apple Crisp with Crunchy Granola Topping	124	1	24	2.9	0	4
26	Watercress and Avocado Salad with Grapefruit Vinaigrette	100	2	14	5.3	0	5
18	White Vegetable Stock	00	00	00	00.0	00	00
64	Whole-Wheat Lasagne with Spinach and Mushrooms	265	17	32	8.7	46	245
45	Whole-Wheat Pizza Dough	159	5	31	2.3	0	94
72	Wild Rice with Dried Cherries and Scallions	170	3.4	30	4.3	10	148
19	Winter Squash Soup	49	1.6	11.2	0.4	0	42
35	Yellow Pepper Sauce	00	00	00	00.0	00	00
35	Yogurt-Cucumber Dressing	12	1	2	0.1	0	7
48	Zucchini and Sun-Dried Tomato Pizza with Mozzarella	237	11	41	4.7	7	178
89	Zucchini-Spinach Frittata	110	12	7.5	3.8	95	143
65	Zucchini Stuffed with Spinach, Ricotta and Parmesan	174	11.8	25	5.0	14	150

Burt Lancaster
mid 1950s

Seated breathing exercises – 1950s

Heirloom Recipes Decalorized

It is not strange, when you really think about it, that family occasions seem always to involve food. Breaking bread/sharing is a tradition that goes back thousands of years. We have all seen sketches of firepits in caves where a successful hunt was being celebrated by a gathering of the clan.

Traditions do not die easily, and the family's favorite foods must not be abandoned just because they are not diet-worthy. They need only be modified.

The term I used in my 1978 book, *Secrets of the Golden Door*, was "decalorized," and that still is the best term. The process need not be completed, and is better not completed, between one event and the next; instead, it should be a gradual but inevitable change. Adjusting recipes during the course of three or four dinners should be enough for successful modification.

I have set aside the following pages for you to mount your most important family recipes, so you can then keep track of the steps you have taken. Your goals are to reduce fats by 50%; to replace white flour carbohydrates with whole grains and to further reduce these by adding bland vegetables such as mushrooms, eggplant and cauliflower; to reduce salt drastically and experiment with doubling the amounts of garlic, onion, herbs or condiments. To cut sugar in half is usually feasible. Cakes or pastries can be sweetened by using reduced (boiled down) fruit juices such as apple juice, cider or cranraspberry juice or pureed bananas, pears or apples.

"No seconds" should become a family refrain, with serving size adjusted according to the size of the person being served. Be bold and innovative. The process of decalorizing requires patience. Each time you prepare the food you will find it easier, and the rewards of a healthy family are truly worth the effort.

D. S.

113

Heirloom Recipes Decalorized

Heirloom Recipes Decalorized

Heirloom Recipes Decalorized

Additional copies may be ordered from the U.S. reservations and administrative office:

Rancho La Puerta, Inc.
Post Office Box 463057
Escondido, California 92046-3057
Attention: Book Orders

Phone U.S. toll-free: (800) 443-7565 or (619) 744-4222

Recipe Index